BEGINNER'S

SERBO-CROATIAN

BEGINNER'S
SERBO-CROATIAN

Duška Radosavljević Heaney

HIPPOCRENE BOOKS, INC.
New York

© 2003 Duška Radosavljević Heaney

All rights reserved.

ISBN 0-7818-0845-6

For information, address:
Hippocrene Books, Inc.
171 Madison Avenue
New York, NY 10016

Cataloging-in-Publication data available from the Library of Congress.

Printed in the United States of America.

CONTENTS

PREFACE

"Quot linguas calles,
tot homines vales."

I believe that it is difficult to learn a language from a book. However, I also believe in the Latin adage that says you are worth as many people as the number of languages you speak. Every effort at addressing the natives of a place one is visiting in the natives' own tongue is always very admirable, and sometimes even crucial.

My chief objective in writing this book has been accessibility and a user-friendly approach. Some linguistic scholars or native language speakers may object to a variety of decisions that I have made. Does Serbo-Croat still exist? Is it the right label? The fact is that the language that was spoken in four of the six republics of the former Yugoslavia was called the Serbo-Croatian language or Serbo-Croat. More or less the same language is still being spoken in those geographical and political units, whatever its name may be. In other words, the reader/user of this book, speaking the language presented here, will be understood in Serbia and Montenegro as well as in Croatia and Bosnia.

The scholarly objections may be aimed at the unsystematic approach to some of the presentation of the language. I have not always stuck to the appropriate linguistic labels, in an attempt not to alienate the reader. In addition, the phonetic principle of four accents in the Serbo-Croatian language—the short rising, the long rising, the short falling, and the long falling—has not received an in-depth explanation in this book. My belief is that the phonetic principles can only be taught orally. Instead, I have attempted to address the pronunciation rules of Serbo-Croat in the introductory section on pronunciation and have applied a transcription technique throughout the lessons.

The reader may choose their own level at which they want to learn the basics of Serbo-Croat. This book contains phrases that the reader will find useful if they wish simply to get by in the language. This is not strictly speaking a phrase book, however, and the reader may find that a phrase they need is not listed in the book. Rather, this book contains explanations and detailed grammatical analysis of the phrases presented in order to aid understanding, memorizing, and flexible and creative use of the language. The reader also can use the more extensive grammar sections simply as a tool for understanding and using the language, or as a more in-depth study of the grammar itself. Serbo-Croatian grammar is not simple and certainly not easy to assimilate without some practice. Application and study is required before the reader is then capable of expressing what they wish on their own.

Each lesson begins with a Serbo-Croatian conversation with side-by-side English translation, followed by an itemized vocabulary and explanations of expressions used, followed by a section on grammar. Each lesson concludes with a listing of useful phrases and a set of exercises. The exercises are designed to help the reader assimilate and use the language and grammar introduced in the given lesson.

The lessons are conceived on the basis of various aspects of human communication—such as getting to know each other, making arrangements and socializing, as well as some aspects of communication related specifically to being a tourist—getting through an airport and booking a hotel room, for example. Simultaneously, each lesson presents a grammatical progression, and often some of the grammar introduced in one lesson will be a prerequisite for understanding the language introduced in the following lessons.

The book also features introductory chapters on the history and culture of the region. In many ways I have envisaged this book as a guidebook through the language and culture of the former Yugoslavia. Inevitably it is an incomplete guidebook and the gaps can only be filled through direct experience of the region. Whether or not you intend to visit the region—enjoy!

Duška Radosavljević Heaney

HISTORY

Early history

Recorded history of the territory covered by the former Yugoslavia dates back to the seventh century B.C. when the ancient Greeks were creating colonies and trading along the Adriatic coast and the territories then inhabited by Illyrian and Thracian tribes. Archaeological findings have revealed evidence of civilization dating back at least to the Bronze Age. Sites in Croatia—Istra and Hvar—date back to 4000 B.C., while a site excavated in 1965 in Lepenski Vir, on the river Danube in Eastern Serbia, dates back to 6000 B.C. Roman sites still survive as cities throughout this area, most notably Dalmatia and Istria in Croatia.

Around the third century B.C. Celtic tribes migrated to the east of the region. At the same time, the Macedonian empire spread in the south of the region and the Roman empire soon began to expand from the west. Tensions between various tribes and empires would last for several centuries. The division of the Roman Empire into Rome and Byzantium in 285 A.D. had a direct effect on the future of the region. The dividing line ran across Montenegro, Bosnia, and Serbia, resulting in the development of distinct cultures on either side of the line.

Driven by the raids of Barbarian tribes, Slavs migrated from the Carpathian Mountains and settled in the Balkan semi-peninsula around the seventh century A.D. They arrived in three groups: Slovenes and Croats inhabited the northern and western region respectively and Serbs settled to the south of the Danube, on the eastern side of the dividing line, between Rome and Byzantium.

Cultural and political development of the South Slavs

Originally the three Slav groups shared the same language and cultural identity but over the centuries they developed distinct cultural and linguistic features. The region that Slovenes inhabited was mostly under Germanic rule and in the sixteenth century the region was incorporated into the Habsburg Empire. In spite of this, the Slovenes retained their Slavic cultural identity. The Slovenian language, however, is now a Slav language distinct from Serbo-Croatian.

The Croats created their first kingdom under King Tomislav in 924, which lasted until 1089 when they fell under Hungarian rule. However, Dalmatia, part of the present-day Croatia, had a different cultural genesis. Originally inhabited by Greeks and Romans, it consequently fell under the control of various powers, but its strongest cultural influence was Venetian, as epitomized by Dubrovnik—one of the most renowned Venetian-style city-states. The Venetian influence lasted from the thirteenth century until the Napoleonic conquest in 1797, when the region was named the Illyrian Province. After a brief French occupation, Dalmatia eventually came under Austrian rule.

The territory of ex-Yugoslav Republic of Bosnia-Herzegovina was originally part of the medieval Hungarian empire. In 1180 it became an independent kingdom under Kulin Ban, characterized by its adoption of a heretic faith—Bogumilism. By the late fourteenth century Bosnia expanded into Serbia and Dalmatia and gained considerable power under the Bosnian King Stefan Tvrtko. With the Turkish invasion in the fifteenth century much of the Bosnian population converted to Islam. By the beginning of the twentieth century this region was also administered by Austria-Hungary.

Following their arrival in the Balkans, the Serbs organized themselves into communities led by chiefs or *župans*. Struggling against the domination of the Byzantine Empire, by the twelfth century Serbia emerged as a powerful kingdom under King Stefan Nemanja who extended his control over Montenegro and parts of present-day Albania. Stefan Nemanja's eldest son Rastko opted for the life of a monk at a monastery on Mount Athos in Greece, where he was renamed Sava. He established the Serbian Orthodox Church in 1219 and built a number of churches in Serbia as well as a Serbian monastery on Mount Athos. Monk Sava became an official Serbian saint—the patron saint of schoolchildren. By the middle of the fourteenth century, Serbia became the greatest and most powerful kingdom in the Balkans under the rule of Stefan Dušan Nemanjić. In 1389 the last Serbian prince, Lazar, led the Serbian army in a battle of resistance against Turkish invasion, which became known as the Battle of Kosovo. The so-called

Golden Age of Serbia, under the rule of the Nemanjić dynasty with the glorious defeat at Kosovo, has often been used as a powerful rhetorical device by the nationalist Serbian politicians of the 1990s. Slobodan Milošević rose to power by addressing the Serbian question of national identity at the 600th anniversary of the Kosovo Battle in 1989.

By 1459 all of Serbia fell under Ottoman rule. This caused great Serbian migrations to Dalmatia, Montenegro, Bosnia, and the Hungarian-controlled region of Vojvodina. The First Serbian Uprising against the Turks, led by Karadjordje (Black George) in 1804, was unsuccessful. Initially supported by Russia, the revolt escalated and failed again when Russia withdrew its troops to fight Napoleon's invasion. Karadjordje emigrated to Austria and his role as the leader of Serbian people was taken over by his friend Miloš Obrenović, who proved more skilled at diplomatic negotiations with the Turks for Serbian independence. The two leaders of Serbian resistance to Turkish domination, Karadjordje Petrović and Miloš Obrenović, became founders of two new Serbian dynasties. The rule of the Obrenović dynasty ended with a coup in 1903 and Petar Karadjordjević, the descendant of Karadjordje, was elected to the throne.

Montenegro emerged as an identifiable geographical and political unit after the Ottoman invasion following the Battle of Kosovo. Its mountainous terrain actually prevented Turkish invasion and, by the end of the fifteenth century, a Montenegrin resistance leader named Ivan Crnojević formed an independent province with a capital in Cetinje. This later became the seat of the Montenegrin dynasty Petrović that originated from a family succession of Bishop-Kings. The most famous Montenegrin Bishop-King and poet, Petar Petrović Njegoš (1830–50), also created some of the greatest masterpieces of Yugoslav literature, *Gorski vijenac* ("The Mountain Wreath") and *Luča mikrokozma* ("The Light of Microcosm"). Following the end of the Turkish Empire, Montenegro received sovereignty and access to the Adriatic Coast at the Congress of Berlin in 1878. The rule of the Petrović dynasty ended in 1916 when the last Montenegrin king Nikola fled to exile under dubious circumstances at the end of his 58-year reign.

The former Yugoslav republic of Macedonia, in the southeast of the region, was initially controlled by Byzantium, and also briefly by the Bulgarians. In the fourteenth century it became part of the Serbian Empire. Following the

Ottoman invasion in the mid-fifteenth century, the region remained under Turkish control until the Balkan Wars in 1912–13 when the Turks were finally expelled. Consequently Greeks, Bulgarians, and Serbs, having all laid claims to this territory, divided it into three parts, as outlined in the treaty of Bucharest in 1913. The name of the region, officially accepted after the Second World War when it became a republic within Yugoslavia, has caused conflict with neighboring Greece due to its links with the region under Philip of Macedon.

Modern history

The European Enlightenment penetrated the Balkan region in the early nineteenth century, resulting in an increased cultural activity. This is when the first theaters, libraries and other cultural institutions opened in Serbia. At the same time, Vuk Stefanović Karadžić, a linguist, ethnographer, and cultural activist, undertook reformation of the Serbian written language on the basis of his research into the actual spoken language on the linguistic territory of Serbo-Croat. He dispensed with the official church script and created a phonetic version, more accessible to the masses. The new alphabet had thirty letters, one for each sound, and corresponded with the rule: "Write as you speak, read as it's written." Following the advice and encouragement of the Slovenian scholar Jernej Kopitar, Vuk Karadžić also collected and recorded Serbian national poetry and prose. These oral epics were at the same time historical records of various events, passed down from generation to generation, and delivered to the accompaniment of the national string instrument—the gusle. On his travels to Vienna, Vuk Karadžić met Goethe, who then translated the Serbian epic *Hasanaginica* into German. This is the period when the also-cosmopolitan Montenegrin Bishop-Prince Njegoš wrote "The Mountain Wreath," and the Croatian linguist Ljudevit Gaj, the leader of the pan-Slavic Illyrian movement, joined efforts with Vuk Karadžić to standardize written Croatian and lay foundations for the Serbo-Croatian language.

On the grounds of the cultural and linguistic similarities that the South Slavs shared, by the end of the nineteenth century the pan-Slavic idea took hold, coinciding with and aiding in the gradual liberation of Slavic regions within the Ottoman and Austro-Hungarian Empires. However, the strength of the movement varied from region to region. Newly liberated Serbia and Montenegro were enthusiastic about unification with the Slavs in the West. Slovenians under Austrian jurisdiction and Croatians under Hungarian rule were divided among themselves as to whether they wanted sole independence or union with the rest of the South Slavs. Following the withdrawal of the Ottomans, Bosnia was annexed by Austria in 1908, and this is where the Illyrian nationalist movement was particularly strong. The hostility to Austro-Hungarian domination, coupled with the movement for independence, led to the assassination on June 28, 1914, of the Austrian Archduke Franz Ferdinand, who had chosen to visit Sarajevo on the holiday that marked the anniversary of the Serbian defeat at Kosovo. The assassination led to the Austrian declaration of war on Serbia and consequently, to the First World War.

By this time, Serbia was a kingdom, the dynasty of Karadjordjević having succeeded the dynasty of Obrenović, following a military coup in 1903 when the unpopular King Aleksandar Obrenović and his mistress were killed. The descendants of Karadjordje had lived in exile. His grandson Petar had married a Montenegrin princess who died in childbirth. Petar Karadjordjević then reared his family in Geneva, maintaining links with the Montenegrin and Russian royals. Restored by popular election to the Serbian throne in 1903, he became a benevolent and popular king. Apart from good statesmanship and military qualities, his credits also included the first translation of John Stuart Mill's essay "On Liberty" in Serbo-Croat. In 1909 he absolved his firstborn son Djordje as heir to the throne in favor of the younger Aleksandar who had displayed a greater degree of self-restraint, responsibility, and a more serious interest in the affairs of the state.

The First World War took Serbia unawares. Having just recovered from the Balkan Wars, the country was not yet ready for another battle. Although the Serbian army resisted Austrian invasion at first, the second attack was stronger and more successful—the Austrian army, fierce weather conditions, and an outbreak of typhoid fever drove the Serbs into retreat. The king and prince led the army on foot across the mountains of Albania to the Ionian Sea where they were taken by the Allies to Greece and France for recuperation before the defense of the Salonica front. Simultaneously, Serbian and Croatian politicians abroad lobbied the Allied powers for the creation of a united South Slavic state following the end of the war. The American president Woodrow Wilson supported the independence of Slavic regions from Austria-Hungary, and the Kingdom of Serbs, Croats, and Slovenes, including Montenegro and Bosnia, was created on December 1, 1918.

Yugoslavia

In 1928 the Kingdom of Serbs, Croats, and Slovenes was renamed Yugoslavia—the Land of the South Slavs. Headed by the Serbian king Aleksandar Karadjordjević, the kingdom was seen by other co-nationals, especially Croats, as a means of Serbian domination. In spite of the king's efforts to please all constituent nations—he even considered making Latin the official alphabet at the expense of Serbian Cyrillics—Croatian resistance caused political tension and anarchy in the parliament, which then led to the dissolution of parliament and the imposition of royal dictatorship. The Yugoslav king Aleksandar Karadjordjević was assassinated in Marseille in 1934, leaving the country in political turmoil in the wake of the Second World War. The heir to the throne was too young to take power and the authority passed to the king's cousin and friend from childhood, Regent Pavle (also referred to as Prince Paul).

The Communist party had been founded in the 1920s. Its membership consisted largely of the developing working classes and peasants from all over the country. At first the party gained considerable support in both the Serbian capital Belgrade and the Croatian capital Zagreb, but it was soon banned by the national government and forced underground, where it worked to establish closer links with the Soviet Union. In 1937 Josip Broz Tito was elected general secretary of the party.

When the Second World War started, Yugoslavia proclaimed itself neutral. By 1941, however, the Italian-German Axis had pushed Prince Paul into official alliance. This caused popular rebellion and a military coup. Consequently Belgrade was bombed on April 6, 1941. German and Italian invasion commenced immediately and, following a short and unsuccessful military resistance, the country was occupied. Germany annexed Slovenia, Italy occupied Montenegro and the Adriatic coast, and Bulgaria took Macedonia. Serbia remained a puppet state and so did Croatia and Bosnia, both of which were controlled by German-appointed Ante Pavelić, the leader of the Croatian pro-Nazi faction Ustaše. In keeping with the Nazi policies, Ustaše were responsible for the extermination of a considerable number of Jews, Gypsies, and Serbs.

The Second World War coincided with a civil war in Yugoslavia. The royal family emigrated to Britain, while the Royalist Army, the *Četniks*, fought both against the Germans and the Communist Partizans. The Partizans, led by Tito, obtained full international support at the expense of the Četniks who had been initially supported by the Allies. Tito established his own government and formed the People's Federal Republic of Yugoslavia in 1943—later renamed Socialist Federal Republic of Yugoslavia. Yugoslavia emerged from the Second World War with great losses, an estimated one-tenth of the population having been killed. However, its borders remained more or less the same, neighboring with Italy to the west, Austria and Hungary to the north, Romania and Bulgaria to the east, Greece to the southeast and Albania to the south.

The transition from monarchy to republic had its own costs. The Communists quickly imposed their authority through intimidation. Private property was confiscated and the "enemies of the people" executed or tried (this included pre-war bourgeoisie, "German collaborators" as well as some theater artists who continued to do their job during the war rather than joining the Partizans). Socialist Federal Republic of Yugoslavia initially followed the Soviet model of political organization, however, in 1948 Yugoslavia was expelled from the Commintern, Tito disassociated himself from Stalin, and developed his own national and international policies. There emerged a Yugoslavian brand of socialism based on the principle of "self-management" whereby control and ownership of the means of production belonged to employees rather than the state.

Meanwhile Tito, Nehru, and Nasser formed the Non-Aligned Movement, by which Yugoslavia became the only Eastern European country not involved in the Cold War. However, some internal problems remained. Yugoslav supporters of Stalin and the USSR were imprisoned on the Goli Otok (Bare Island) where they underwent ideological reeducation through harsh treatment. This continued until the early 1950s. From this period on, two currents gradually emerged within the Yugoslav League of Communists—a conservative and a more liberal one. Tito fluctuated between the two. The

1960s were marked by a thriving economic development, which in the 1970s led to a strengthening movement for greater economic and political autonomy of the richer republics, such as Croatia and Slovenia. In addition, the 1974 constitution introduced greater decentralization and an increased autonomy of individual republics. By this constitution two regions within Serbia— Vojvodina and Kosovo—were also given the status of autonomous regions.

Since 1974, the Socialist Federal Republic of Yugoslavia consisted of six republics and two autonomous provinces within Serbia, the largest of the republics. Apart from the six major nations in each republic, there were many national minorities living in Yugoslavia, including Albanians, Hungarians, Romanians, Slovaks, Romanies, Turks, and Italians. The most important policy of socialist Yugoslavia was equality and the "brotherhood and unity" of all peoples living in the country. This was reflected in all federal and republic institutions that always endeavored to include representatives from each ethnic group. All ethnic groups had a right to official education, culture and the media in their own language and a right to practice their own religion, although religion as such was not encouraged by the socialist system. Indeed, the socialist years saw a considerable degree of intermarriage between various religious and ethnic groups, particularly in Bosnia where an impressive ethnic mix coincided with a strong socialist allegiance.

Following Tito's death in 1980 and an economic crisis in the early 1980s, ethnic problems resurfaced, with individual republics pushing for more autonomy and individual ethnic groups pushing for more recognition. The richer republics felt disadvantaged at having to finance the poorer ones; the Serbs, dispersed by communist geographical reorganization saw themselves as threatened—especially the Serbs in Kosovo who feared an increasingly violent Albanian movement for Kosovo independence. The tension finally culminated with a formation of various nationalist movements within the country. The Serbian nationalist Slobodan Milošević rose to power by withdrawing the autonomy from Kosovo and Vojvodina that had been granted to them in 1974. His Croatian counterpart Franjo Tudjman won the elections soon after and, restoring some of the nationalist Croatian symbols such as the checkered flag, pressed for Croatian secession. Slovenia had seceded relatively easily, however, the existence of a considerable Serbian population in Croatia made Croatian secession more problematic. Similarly the ethnic mix in Bosnia made Bosnian secession even more complicated. This finally led to one of the most terrible wars in Europe since the Second World War.

The 1995 Dayton Peace Agreement ended the war in Bosnia, but Slobodan Milošević's troubles at home continued. Having lost the local elections in 1996, Milošević attempted to annul the results, bringing the increasingly discontent and impoverished people of Serbia out on the streets. The peaceful, student-led demonstrations against Milošević quickly increased in number, team spirit, and good humor, continuing daily for three months in the winter of 1996–97. The opposition coalition finally gained their seats, but disintegrated quickly thereafter, effectively leaving Milošević still in power. In his last bid to secure his position by diverting public attention to "outside enemies," Milošević turned to the Kosovo problem, which had been simmering ever since his glorious ascent ten years previously. An increased activity of the Albanian separatist organization—the Kosovo Liberation Army (KLA)—and frequent clashes between the Serbian police and the KLA caused a direct international involvement. Unsuccessful negotiations for the future of Kosovo finally led to the devastating NATO bombing of Yugoslavia in 1999.

More than ten years of Slobodan Milošević's dictatorship ended on October 5, 2000, following a general election and a brief "Bulldozer Revolution." The consequent inauguration of Vojislav Koštunica as president of Yugoslavia marked a turning point in the modern history of the region, hopefully putting an end to the post-socialist violence and corruption, and opening up new horizons. Yugoslavia has also begun a period of reintegration within the wider context of Europe.

At the time of writing, the Federal Republic of Yugoslavia still consists of Serbia and Montenegro, although negotiations regarding the nature of the federation are under way.

Under international pressure and with the promise of reconstruction aid, Milošević was finally arrested by the new Yugoslav authorities in April 2001 and delivered to the Hague tribunal, where his trial is under way at publication time. Even more recently, through international mediation, Yugoslavia has been renamed the Union of Serbia and Montenegro, signifying and increasingly loosening nature of the federation.

THE SERBO-CROATIAN LANGUAGE

Origins and geography of the language

Slavonic (or Slavic) languages belong to the Indo-European family of languages and divide into three groups: East Slavonic languages such as Russian, Byelorussian, and Ukrainian, West Slavonic languages such as Polish, Czech, and Slovak, and the South Slavonic group of languages consisting of Serbo-Croat, Slovenian, Macedonian, and Bulgarian.

All South Slavonic languages originated from the same language which, in the course of history, developed into distinct linguistic units. Serbo-Croat and Slovenian belong to the Western South Slavonic unit and Macedonian and Bulgarian to the Eastern South Slavonic unit. The Eastern South Slavonic unit also includes the first literary Slavonic language, dating from the ninth century A.D.—the Old Slavonic language—based on a Macedonian dialect spoken in the region of Salonica. Old Slavonic is now a dead language, having formed a basis for the development of other literary languages in the South Slavonic group of languages.

The Serbo-Croatian language—or Serbo-Croat—was the official name of the language spoken in most of the Socialist Federal Republic of Yugoslavia. The other two main Yugoslav languages were Slovenian and Macedonian, while major ethnic minorities such as Albanians or Hungarians had a right to official education, culture, and the media in their own languages.

There were slight dialectal differences between varieties of Serbo-Croat spoken in Serbia, Croatia, Bosnia, and Montenegro; however, these were accommodated under the umbrella of a single language, as various peoples could generally understand each other.

Dialects and varieties within Serbo-Croat

The Serbo-Croatian language therefore had three dialects: *štokavski* (or the "*shto*-dialect"), *kajkavski* (or the "*kaj*-dialect"), and *čakavski* (or the "*cha*-dialect"). *Što*, *kaj*, and *ča* are different forms of the pronoun "what" in three Croatian dialects. The *štokavski* dialect was the most widespread dialect spoken in Croatia, as well as on the entire Serbo-Croatian linguistic territory. In the nineteenth century, the *shto*-dialect was chosen by the Serbian language reformer Vuk Karadžić and the Croatian Ljudevit Gaj as the basis for the standardized literary Serbo-Croatian language.

There are three varieties within the *štokavski* dialect ("ekavica," "ijekavica," and "ikavica") that originate from various pronunciations of the Old Slavonic letter ʙ called the "yat" and the equivalent of the letter "e." Therefore, for example, the word *mleko* (milk) is pronounced in three different ways:

mleko   mlijeko   mliko

In the *ekavica* dialect the Old Slavonic "e" has become short (mleko), in *ijekavica* it has remained long "ije" (mlijeko), and in *ikavica* it has turned into "i" (mliko). The "ekavica" is spoken in Serbia (and Macedonia), the "ijekavica" is spoken in most of Croatia, Bosnia, and Montenegro, and the "ikavica" is spoken in parts of Bosnia and Croatia. The "ekavica" and "ijekavica" are used in literature.

There are also slight differences in vocabulary among various regions, which are for the most part mutually understandable. For example:

Croatian "dom" = Serbian "kuća" (home)
But note:
Croatian "kućanica" = Serbian "domaćica" (housewife)

Serbo-Croat today

Following the disintegration of Yugoslavia, the language spoken in Croatia became known as Croatian, the language spoken in Bosnia as Bosnian and the language spoken in Serbia as Serbian. All three languages have undergone some attempts at reconstruction of vocabulary to differentiate themselves from Serbo-Croat. Most significantly in Croatia, these attempts resemble those undertaken by the French linguists in order to resist or revert English penetration of the French language, and involve coinage of new words on the basis of existing ones. Alternatively, in Bosnia and Serbia, some more archaic or localized synonyms for existing words were brought into everyday and literary use. However, these changes haven't quite taken root yet. Although Serbo-Croat is decreasingly referred to as an existing language, it is the label, rather than the language itself, that has gone out of use.

In spite of the currently debatable nature of the notion of Serbo-Croatian language, I have decided to refer to the language presented in this book as Serbo-Croat. The terms Serbo-Croatian and Serbo-Croat can be used interchangeably. In this book, the term Serbo-Croatian is used where the term clearly has the function of an adjective and accompanies a noun, such as "the Serbo-Croatian language," "Serbo-Croatian words," etc. The term Serbo-Croat is used in more general terms, where the term stands for the name of the language, such as "in Serbo-Croat, nouns have seven cases," etc.

However, in keeping with the tendency to refer to languages in their adjectival form in the English language (e.g. English, Spanish, German, etc.), the title of this book remains Beginner's Serbo-Croatian. This would also, hopefully, go some way towards distinguishing the actual language from its old label—Serbo-Croat—which might have been more commonly associated with the official language of the socialist Yugoslavia. For practical purposes the use of the term Serbo-Croat within the book was maintained, without any political connotations whatsoever.

SERBO-CROATIAN PHONETICS

There are 5 vowels (**a**, **e**, **i**, **o**, **u**) and 25 consonants in the Serbo-Croatian language. The only consonant that can be used as a vowel is **r** (in words such as *vrt* "garden" and *prst* "finger"). All vowels are clear and can be either short or long depending on their position in a word. The stress is often on the first syllable (BER-lin, rather than Ber-LIN). In long words the stress is near the first syllable (as in Ah-MEH-ri-ka). All vowels and consonants are pronounced at all times. There are no diphthongs in Serbo-Croat.

Serbo-Croat is written in both the Latin and Cyrillic alphabets. The Latin alphabet is used in the western parts of the former Yugoslavia, such as Croatia and Slovenia, and the Cyrillic is used in Serbia, Montenegro, and exclusively in the Former Yugoslav Republic of Macedonia (FYR Macedonia). The Latin alphabet, based on the Western model, is called *Abeceda*, and the Cyrillic alphabet, based on the Greek model, is called *Azbuka*. While the order of letters in the two alphabets is different, each has thirty letters, where each letter corresponds to a particular sound. Serbo-Croat is therefore a phonetic language and very easy to read.

Cyrillic alphabet

Азбука	Azbuka	
(Cyrillic letter)	(Latin equivalent)	(pronunciation)

А, а	A, a	father, never as in ace
Б, б	B, b	be
В, в	V, v	very
Г, г	G, g	great, never as in George
Д, д	D, d	do
Ђ, ђ	Dj, dj	dy, as in dew in Br. English
Е, е	E, e	men, never as in East
Ж, ж	Ž, ž	zh, as in treasure
З, з	Z, z	zoo
И, и	I, i	ink, never as in side
Ј, ј	J, j	yes, never as in jug
К, к	K, k	kind
Л, л	L, l	love
Љ, љ	Lj, lj	ly, as in allure
М, м	M, m	mother
Н, н	N, n	next
Њ, њ	Nj, nj	ny, as in lasagne
О, о	O, o	door or orange, never as in go or out
П, п	P, p	pot
Р, р	R, r	room
С, с	S, s	some, never as in sure
Т, т	T, t	tall
Ћ, ћ	Ć, ć	ty or soft ch, as in gotcha!
У, у	U, u	school or push, never as in united
Ф, ф	F, f	fast
Х, х	H, h	hero
Ц, ц	C, c	ts as in lots, never as in car
Ч, ч	Č, č	hard ch, as in chair
Џ, џ	DŽ, dž	hard j or g, as in judge
Ш, ш	Š, š	sh as in shoe

Latin alphabet

Abeceda	Examples (Latin)	(Cyrillic)	Pronunciation	Translation
A, a	aerodrom	аеродром	AH-ehrod-rom	airport
B, b	biti	бити	BIT-ti	to be
C, c	car	цар	tzar	tzar
Č, č	čaj	чај	chah-y	tea
Ć, ć	ćup	ћуп	tyoup	jug
D, d	dan	дан	daan	day
DŽ, dž	džez	џез	dzhez	jazz
Dj, dj	djak	ђак	dyak	pupil, schoolchild
E, e	eho	ехо	EH-khoh	echo
F, f	funta	фунта	FOON-tah	pound
G, g	gost	гост	gohost	guest
H, h	hvala	хвала	khVAA-lah	thank you
I, i	izlaz	излаз	IZ-laz	exit
J, j	jug	југ	youg	south
K, k	kolači	колачи	kol-LAACHi	cakes
L, l	lav	лав	lav	lion
Lj, lj	ljubav	љубав	LYOU-bav	love
M, m	molim	молим	MOL-lim	please
N, n	ništa	ништа	NISH-tah	nothing
Nj, nj	Njujork	Њујорк	NYOUY-york	New York
O, o	oblak	облак	OB-blak	cloud
P, p	pošta	пошта	POSH-ta	post office/mail
R, r	restoran	ресторан	rest-TOR-rann	restaurant
S, s	slika	слика	SLIK-kah	picture
Š, š	šah	шах	shahh	chess
T, t	taksi	такси	TAK-si	taxi
U, u	ulaz	улаз	OU-laz	entrance
V, v	voda	вода	VOD-dah	water
Z, z	zdravo	здраво	ZDRAV-voh	hello
Ž, ž	život	живот	ZHI-vot	life

Pronunciation and transcription

- Vowels are always clear sounding (like ah, eh, eeh, oh, oo where "h" is silent). Pronunciation can be either short or long like the sound "a" in cut or father, "e" in men or hey, "i" in it or eel, "o" in orange or door, and "u" in put or pool.

- C is never pronounced as "k" but only as a single sound similar to "ts" or "tz."

- Č and ć are similarly produced, but č ("tch") is harder than ć (which sounds more like "ty" or "ch"). Surname endings -ić and -vić are pronounced as soft "ich" or "vich."

   Therefore, *Marković* is quite distinct from *Markovič* and is never pronounced as "Markovik." Similarly, *Caričić* would be pronounced as "Tsarichich," whereby the first "ch" (*č*) is harder than the second "ch" (*ć*).

- The letters dž and dj each correspond to a single sound and are represented by single letters in the Cyrillic alphabet. The two sounds are produced similarly but differ in softness, dž sounding like "dzh" and dj like "dy." The letter dj also appears in print as đ or capital Đ. Both are correct but the latter is more common in handwriting and the former in typewriting.

- H is more aspirated and never silent in Serbo-Croatian words.

Although it is relatively easy to read Serbo-Croat once the basic rules of pronunciation are learned, I have devised a transcription method to aid the reader's memorization of particular words and phrases. Words are divided into syllables on the basis of emphasis (see pronunciation, the Latin alphabet, above), rather than on the basis of the grammatically proper syllable division in Serbo-Croat. For example, the word *restoran* is properly divided as "res-to-ran"; however, for pronunciation purposes I have divided it as "rest-TOR-ran," doubling the letters "t" and "r" to point out the emphasis and the shortness of the vowel "o." The syllable spelled in capital letters represents the stressed syllable. Note that the emphasis in Serbo-Croatian pronunciation is different from American pronunciation where the emphasis in this word is on the first syllable. (Notice also, for example, that New York is pronounced as one word in Serbo-Croat, whereby the emphasis is on the first syllable and both vowels are considerably shorter than in English.)

In the transcriptions, lowercase letters therefore indicate unstressed syllables. Some words in Serbo-Croat are never stressed but pronounced as part of the adjacent word. In this case, I have connected the unstressed words to the other words with a hyphen. For example:

Kako ste?
(KAKkoh-steh)
How are you?

VOWELS

- short **a**, if not followed by a consonant, is marked as **ah**, and a long **a** as **aa** or **aah**

- short **e**, if not followed by a consonant, is marked as **eh**, and a long **e** as **ei** or **ey**

- short **i**, if not followed by a consonant, is marked as **ih**, and a long **i** as **ee**

- short **o** will remain **o** if followed by a consonant or else it is marked as **oh**, and a long **o** is marked as **oho**

- short **u** is marked as **u** or **ou** in most cases, and long **u** is transcribed as **oo**

CONSONANTS

- **h** is accompanied by **k** or another **h** to differentiate it from silent **h** used to determine pronunciation of other sounds

- some consonants are doubled in transcription to determine the shortness of surrounded vowels (as in "rest-TOR-rann")

- typically Serbo-Croatian consonants, such as č, ć, etc. are transcribed as explained in the pronunciation notes above

N.B. It is assumed gradually that the reader has learned to pronounce certain short words which are frequently used, and the transcription is applied selectively to new and longer words.

Exercises

I. Transliterate the following into Serbo-Croatian Latin script, then translate:

кока-кола

Америка

фудбал

1 долар

Џорџ Вашингтон

Мекдоналдс

Београд

II. Transliterate the following words into Serbo-Croatian Latin and Cyrillic:

New York

taxi

restaurant

rent-a-car

American Express

London

ABBREVIATIONS

acc.	accusative
adj.	adjective
adv.	adverb
cl.	class (of verbs)
coll. n.	collective noun
dat.	dative
def. adj.	definite adjective
fem.	feminine gender
gen.	genitive
ijek.	*ijekavica* (see varieties of Serbo-Croat)
inf.	infinitive
instr.	instrumental
lit.	literally
masc.	masculine gender
n.	noun
neut.	neuter gender
nom.	nominative
p.	person
pl.	plural
pl. tantum	pluralia tantum
poss. adj.	possessive adjective
prep.	prepositional
sbd	somebody
sing.	singular
sth	something
v.	verb
voc.	vocative

LESSON
ONE

DIALOGUE

Predstavljanje

STJUARDESA:	Poštovani putnici, dobrodošli na let Njujork—Beograd. Posada JAT-a želi vam srećan i ugodan put.
MARKO:	Izvinite, vi ste Jugosloveni?
ROBERT:	Ja sam Francuz, moja supruga je Jugoslovenka.
JELENA:	Jeste li vi Jugosloven?
MARKO:	Moji roditelji su Jugosloveni, ja sam Amerikanac.
JELENA:	Ja sam Jelena, ovo je Robert.
MARKO:	Ja sam Marko. Drago mi je.
ROBERT:	Idete li za Beograd?
MARKO:	Idem na more. A vi?
JELENA:	Robert ide poslovno za Beograd.
MARKO:	Šta vi radite, Roberte?
ROBERT:	Ja sam profesor informatike. Idem u Beograd na konferenciju. A vi?
MARKO:	Ja sam ekonomista. A vi Jelena?
JELENA:	Ja sam lekar.
MARKO:	Vi, Roberte, dobro govorite srpskohrvatski.
ROBERT:	Hvala. Ja dobro govorim, a ništa ne razumem!
	(Smeh.)

Introductions

STEWARDESS: Dear passengers, welcome on board the flight New York—
Belgrade. The JAT crew wishes you a happy and comfort-
able journey.

MARKO: Excuse me, you are Yugoslavs?

ROBERT: I am French, my wife is a Yugoslav.

JELENA: Are you Yugoslav?

MARKO: My parents are Yugoslavian, I am an American.

JELENA: I am Jelena, this is Robert.

MARKO: I am Marko. Pleased to meet you.

JELENA: Are you going to Belgrade?

MARKO: I am going to the seaside. And you?

JELENA: Robert is going on business to Belgrade.

MARKO: What do you do, Robert?

ROBERT: I am an Information Technology lecturer. I am going to a
conference in Belgrade. And you?

MARKO: I am an accountant. And you, Jelena?

JELENA: I am a physician.

MARKO: You speak good Serbo-Croat, Robert.

ROBERT: Thank you. I speak well, but I understand nothing!

              (Laughter.)

VOCABULARY

Amerikanac	an American
dobro	well, good
dobrodošli	welcome
drago mi je	pleased to meet you
ekonomista	economist, accountant
Francuz	Frenchman
govoriti	to speak
hvala	thank you
i	and
ići	to go
informatika	information science, IT
izvini/izvinite	excuse me
JAT (jugoslovenski aero transport)	Yugoslav Air Transport
Jugosloven/i	Yugoslav/s
konferencija	conference
lekar	doctor, general practitioner, physician
let	flight
leteti	to fly
moj,-a,-e	my
more	sea, seaside
na	on, to
ništa	nothing
ovo	this
pa	then
posada	crew
poslovno	on business
poštovan	respected
profesor	teacher, lecturer, professor
put	journey
putnik/putnici	passenger/s, traveler/s
raditi	to do
razumeti	to understand
roditelj/i	parent/s
samo	only, just

smeh	laughter
srećan	happy
srpskohrvatski	Serbo-Croat, Serbo-Croatian language
stjuardesa	stewardess
supruga	wife
šta	what
ugodan	comfortable
za	for, to
želeti	to wish

EXPLANATIONS

- *Ja sam Jugosloven. A vi?* I am a Yugoslav. And (what about) you?

The word *a* can be translated as either "and" or "but." It is used to introduce a new subject, as in the example above, or to point out a contrast:

Ja sam Jugosloven, a vi ste Francuz. I am a Yugoslav but you are a Frenchman.

- *Ja sam Jelena, ovo je Robert.* I am Jelena, this is Robert.

The demonstrative pronoun *ovo* is used to point to something near the subject or to introduce someone or something new. This is referred to as "introductory *ovo*."

- *A vi, Roberte?* And you, Robert?

The declension of nouns in Serbo-Croat has seven cases. These cases correspond to the function of the noun in a sentence. Personal names as well as all other nouns must be declined and accordingly take the required endings for each case. *Roberte* with an "e" at the end is the vocative form of Robert. The vocative case is used for addressing or calling someone. Some personal names that end in a vowel, such as Jelena or Marko, do not change form in the vocative case.

- *Ja sam Amerikanac.* I am an American.

Moji roditelji su Amerikanci. My parents are Americans.

In some nouns ending with a consonant, the consonant is preceded by a "fleeting a," an "a" which disappears in other forms of the noun. For example, the plural of *Amerikanac* is *Amerikanci*.

- *Idem za Beograd.* I am going to Belgrade.

Idem u Beograd. I am going to Belgrade.

Idem na more. I am going to the seaside.

The first expression—with the preposition *za*—is used specifically when traveling. *Za* indicates the destination of movement and is only used with names of places: *Idem za Beograd.* Its meaning corresponds most closely with the English preposition "for," or in this particular context, "towards."

The second expression—with the preposition *u*—is used more frequently and more generally with the name of a place or a country. The meaning of *u* corresponds most closely to the English preposition "in" or "into."

The third expression—with the preposition *na*—is used when referring to a geographical location such as the seaside, or specific mountains, lakes, or rivers. *Na* corresponds most closely to the English preposition "on" or "onto."

The expression *idem za/u/na* . . . requires a particular case of the noun called the accusative. The accusative is the fifth case and answers the question "whom / what (do I see)?" Masculine and neuter nouns such as *Beograd* and *more* stay the same in the accusative case because of their gender. The noun *konferencija* changes in the accusative because it is feminine in gender.

Idem na konferenciju. I am going to a conference.

The case declensions will be described in more detail throughout the book. The accusative singular case is discussed in Lesson Two.

- *Ništa ne razumem.* I don't understand anything. (lit.: I do not understand nothing.)

The Serbo-Croatian language features double negation as a grammatically correct form of negation. Here *ništa* meaning "nothing" appears together with the negative form *ne razumem* meaning "I don't understand."

GRAMMAR

Articles

There are no articles in the Serbo-Croatian language. The noun *profesor* can mean "a professor" or "the professor" depending on context.

Personal pronouns

	singular	*plural*
1st p.	ja (I)	mi (we)
2nd p.	ti (you)	vi (you)
3rd p.	on (he)	oni (they/masculine)
	ona (she)	one (they/feminine)
	ono (it)	ona (they/neuter)

Ja (I) is only spelled with a capital "J" at the beginning of a sentence. At all other times it is spelled *ja*.

Oni su Jugosloveni, ja sam Amerikanac. They are Yugoslavs, I am an American.

When addressing someone formally or politely—an older person or a stranger—the second-person plural pronoun is used:

Šta vi radite, Jelena? What do you do, Jelena?

In writing, particularly in correspondence, this would be spelled with a capital "V": *Šta Vi radite, Jelena?*

Nouns

Nouns in Serbo-Croat are masculine, feminine, or neuter in gender, and singular or plural in number. Nouns are declined in seven cases in both singular and plural forms.

Masculine nouns

Masculine nouns often end with a consonant:

Jugosloven (Yugoslav); *putnik* (passenger); *profesor* (professor)

The plural form of masculine nouns is created most often by adding the suffix *-i*:

Jugosloveni (Yugoslavs); *profesori* (professors)

This is not always the case, however, and the exceptions will be discussed as they arise in the lessons (e.g. the masculine noun *sat* (clock) in Lesson Three).

Some male personal names or words of foreign origin that have been attributed masculine gender end in *-a*, *-o*, or *-e*:

Saša, Marko, Pavle, radio, video, auto (from automobile)

Feminine nouns

Feminine nouns typically end with *-a*:

stjuardesa (stewardess); *Jugoslovenka* (a Yugoslav woman); *Jelena*

In the plural form feminine nouns often end with *-e*:

stjuardese; Jugoslovenke

Rarely do feminine nouns end in a consonant. Such exceptions will be indicated as they arise (e.g. the feminine noun *noć* ["night"] in Lesson Four).

Neuter nouns

The neuter gender often applies to children, young animals, and, not exclusively, to objects. Objects can be of all genders, unlike in English where they are always neuter (referred to as "it"). Neuter nouns in Serbo-Croat often end in -*e*:

dete (child); *jagnje* (lamb); *more* (sea); *dugme* (button)

Neuter nouns can also end with -*o*:

čelo (forehead); *selo* (village)

In the plural form, neuter nouns typically end with -*a*:

deca (children); *mora* (seas); *sela* (villages)

Some neuter nouns end exceptionally with a consonant in the plural form:

jagnjad (lambs); *dugmad* (buttons)

Certain nouns in Serbo-Croat have "dual" or "common" gender. These are generally masculine nouns that can also represent feminine gender.

On je profesor, a ona je lekar. He is a professor, and she is a physician.

On je lekar, a ona je profesor. He is a physician, and she is a professor.

N.B. Nationality is always expressed as a masculine or feminine noun (depending on the subject):

Ja sam Francuz.
Ona je Amerikanka.

Unlike in English where it can be either a noun or an adjective:

I am a Frenchman. Or: I am French.
She is an American. Or: She is American.

Adjectives

Adjectives always correspond with the gender and case of the noun they are describing or modifying. They also agree with the noun in number (singular or plural). The noun generally follows the adjective in word order.

srećan Amerikanac a happy American (masc. sing.)
srećni Amerikanci happy Americans (masc. pl.)

srećna Jugoslovenka a happy Yugoslav woman (fem. sing.)
srećne Jugoslovenke happy Yugoslav women (fem. pl.)

srećno dete a happy child (neut. sing.)
srećna deca* happy children (neut. pl.)

*The noun *dete* has an irregular plural form. It is best memorized this way.

Possessive adjective *moj, moja, moje* "my"

The possessive adjective "my" agrees with the gender of the noun that it accompanies in the same way as other adjectives.

Moj suprug je Francuz. My husband is a Frenchman. (masc. sing.)
Moja supruga je Jugoslovenka. My wife is a Yugoslav. (fem. sing.)
Moje dete je srećno. My child is happy. (neut. sing.)
Moji roditelji su Amerikanci. My parents are Americans. (masc. pl.)

Verbs

Verbs can be divided into several categories depending on their function and usage in the sentence. For example, principal verbs express an action or a state and auxiliary verbs serve to make up other tenses and grammatical structures. The verb *biti* (to be) is often used as an auxiliary verb just as in English. Verbs can also be described as transitive if they require an object (such as "to accuse" in English) or as reflexive if the object of the verb is at the same time the subject (such as *češljati se* "to comb one's own hair, to groom oneself").

Verbs in Serbo-Croat are conjugated and take various endings for each person in singular or plural form in the different tenses.

Id__ete__ li za Beograd? Are you going to Belgrade?
Id__em__ na more. I am going to the sea.

Serbo-Croatian verbs divide into six classes on the basis of their morphology and the kinds of endings that they take in their various inflections. This classification is important for the purposes of building various grammatical structures and tenses. The six classes will be discussed one by one (most significantly in Lessons Five and Six). At first, however, verbs will be discussed individually. Their changes through person and number in a particular tense—their conjugation—and their category (or class) will be indicated. In this way, the different classes of verbs are introduced gradually in separate lessons and in conjunction with particular examples.

Sixth-class verbs are the most common. Some sixth-class verbs are introduced below.

Present tense of *govoriti* "to speak" and *raditi* "to do"

The verbs *govoriti* (to speak) and *raditi* (to do, to work) belong to the sixth class of verbs. The verbs of the sixth class have the ending *-i* in the third-person singular of the present tense:

Ona radi. She works.
Ona govori. She speaks.

They take the ending *-e* (long "e") in the third-person plural of the present tense:

Oni rade. They work.
Oni govore. They speak.

Present tense conjugations of *govoriti* (to speak) and *raditi* (to do):

singular	*plural*
ja govorim (I speak)	mi govorimo (we speak)
ti goviriš (you speak)	vi govorite (you speak)
on/ona/ono govori̯ (he/she/it speaks)	oni/one/ona govore̯ (they speak)

ja radim (I do)	mi radimo (we do)
ti radiš (you do)	vi radite (you do)
on/ona/ono radi̯ (he/she/it does)	oni/one/ona rade̯ (they do)

Present tense of *ići* "to go"

Most other classes of verbs take the ending *-e* in the third-person singular of the present tense and the ending *-u* in the third-person plural of the present tense. *Ići* (to go) belongs to the first class of verbs. (The first-class verbs are introduced in more detail in Lesson Four.)

singular	*plural*
idem (I go)	idemo (we go)
ideš (you go)	idete (you go)
ide̯ (he/she/it goes)	idu̯ (they go)

It is not always necessary to use the pronoun before the verb. The ending of the verb indicates whether it is in the first, second, or third-person singular or plural form.

(Ja) Idem na more. I am going to the sea.
(Oni) Idu u Beograd. They are going to Belgrade.

N.B. There is no difference between the simple present and the present progressive tense in the Serbo-Croatian language. Therefore, *ja govorim* can mean either "I speak" or "I am speaking," depending on context.

Jesam: The present tense of *biti* "to be"

Biti (to be) is an irregular verb that functions as an auxiliary (as in English).

The verb *jesam* is itself a defective verb because it only has a present tense conjugation. *Jesam* corresponds with the present tense of the verb *biti* (to be), and conjugates as follows:

ja jesam (I am)	mi jesmo (we are)
ti jesi (you are)	vi jeste (you are)
on/ona/ono jeste (he . . . is)	oni/one/ona jesu (they are)

Jesam also has a more commonly used short form:

ja sam	mi smo
ti si	vi ste
on/ona/ono je	oni/one/ona su

In speech, the long forms of the verb *jesam* are stressed. The short forms are unstressed—they are called "enclitics." Enclitics usually follow a stressed word in a sentence, specifically a noun or a pronoun. They never stand on their own (without a subject), and cannot be used at the beginning of a sentence. The third-person singular *je* is the only exception—its use at the beginning of a sentence will be discussed below.

Ja sam Amerikanac. I am an American.
Oni su Jugosloveni. They are Yugoslavs.

Question formation

There are several ways to form questions in Serbo-Croat. Here we shall examine two ways:

• Turning a statement into a question by raising the intonation.

   Vi ste Jugosloveni? You are Yugoslavs?

- Using the verb followed by the interrogative particle *li* to make a question.

Govori li on engleski? Does he speak English?

The affirmative word order (subject + verb + object) is thus inverted:

verb + *li* + (subject) + object

The subject may not always be necessary since the form of the verb implies it:

Idete li za Beograd? Are you going to Belgrade?

In the case of the present tense of the verb "to be," *jesam*, the long forms of the verb are used to form a question:

Jeste li vi Jugosloven? Are you a Yugoslav?
Jesu li oni Amerikanci? Are they Americans?

Exception: When asking the question in the third-person singular, the short form is used:

Je li ovo Jelena? Is this Jelena?
Je li on profesor? Is he a professor?

In this case of the third-person singular, the short form *je* (is) is stressed in pronunciation.

USEFUL PHRASES

Pronunciation is given in parentheses. The accent is on the capitalized syllables. Hyphenated words are pronounced together.

Izvinite, ja sam Amerikanac. Govorite li engleski?
(IzVEEnitteh, YAH-sam AhmerriKAANnats. GOVvorritteh-lee EHNglesskih)
Excuse me, I am an American (man). Do you speak English?

Ja sam Amerikanka.
(YAH-sam AhmeRIKankah)
I am an American (woman).

Jeste li vi Yugosloven?
(YESste-lee VEE YuggosSLOVven)
Are you a Yugoslav?

Idete li za Beograd? / Letite li za Beograd?
(IDetteh-lee zah behOGgrad) / (LETtitte-lee za behOGgrad)
Are you going to Belgrade? / Are you flying to Belgrade?

Dobro govorite engleski.
(DOBbroh GOVvorritteh EHNglesskih)
You speak good English.

Ne razumem srpski.
(neh-razZOOMmem srpskih)
I don't understand Serbian.

Drago mi je. / Drago mi je da smo se upoznali.
(DRAHgoh-mee-yeh) / (DRAHgoh-mee-yeh da-smoh-seh OOpozznalih)
Pleased to meet you. / Pleased to have met you.

Srećan put!
(SRECHan poot)
Happy journey. (Have a nice safe trip.)

Nationalities

Australijanac, Australijanka, Australijanci
Australian (man), (woman), Australians

Bosanac, Bosanka, Bosanci
Bosnian (man), (woman), Bosnians

Crnogorac, Crnogorka, Crnogorci
Montenegrin (man), (woman), Montenegrins

Englez, Engleskinja, Englezi
Englishman, Englishwoman, English (pl.)

Hrvat, Hrvatica, Hrvati
Croat (man), (woman), Croats

Irac, Irkinja, Irci
Irishman, Irishwoman, Irish (pl.)

Kanadjanin, Kanadjanka, Kanadjani
Canadian (man), (woman), Canadians

Makedonac, Makedonka, Makedonci
Macedonian (man), (woman), Macedonians

Nemac, Nemica, Nemci
German (man), (woman), Germans

Slovenac, Slovenka, Slovenci
Slovenian (man), (woman), Slovenes

Srbin, Srpkinja, Srbi
Serb (man), (woman), Serbs

Španac, Španjolka, Španci
Spaniard (man), (woman), Spaniards

EXERCISES

I. Translate into English.

   1. Ja sam Amerikanac, a vi?
   2. Oni su Francuzi.
   3. Ovo je Jelena. Ona je Jugoslovenka.
   4. Mi govorimo srpski.
   5. Govorite li vi engleski?
   6. Idemo na more.
   7. Ide li ona za Beograd?
   8. Šta vi radite?
   9. Je li stjuardesa dobra?
  10. Moja supruga je srećna.

II. Turn these questions into statements.

   e.g.: Govorite li srpskohrvatski?—Vi govorite srpskohrvatski.

   1. Jeste li vi Francuz?
   2. Idete li na more?
   3. Je li on profesor?
   4. Govorite li francuski?
   5. Jesu li deca dobra?

III. Turn these statements into questions.

   e.g.: Moj suprug je dobar.—Je li moj suprug dobar?

   1. Ovo je Jelena.
   2. On je Amerikanac.
   3. Moja deca su srećna.
   4. Moji roditelji su Amerikanci.
   5. Stjuardesa je Jugoslovenka.

IV. Translate into Serbo-Croat.

1. We are happy Americans.
2. He is French, and you?
3. She is a Yugoslav.
4. Do they speak English?
5. He speaks Serbo-Croat.
6. This is the stewardess. She speaks English.
7. My children are good.
8. He is going to the sea.
9. We are going to New York.
10. Are you going to New York?

LESSON
TWO

DIALOGUE

Učtivosti – Usluge

STJUARDESA:	Dobar dan. Kako ste?
SVI:	Dobar dan. Dobro, hvala.
STJUARDESA:	Želite li piće?
MARKO:	Ko želi piće? Jelena? Roberte?
JELENA i ROBERT:	Da!
STJUARDESA:	Izvolite, šta želite?
MARKO:	Jelena, šta vi želite?
JELENA:	Jednu kafu za mene, molim.
STJUARDESA:	Belu ili crnu?
JELENA:	Belu kafu bez šećera.
MARKO:	A vi, Roberte? Hoćete li jedno pivo?
ROBERT:	Ne, hvala. Izvinite, šta još imate?
STJUARDESA:	Čaj, voćni sok . . .
ROBERT:	Jedan sok od ananasa, molim.
STJUARDESA:	Žao mi je ali sok od ananasa nemamo. Sok od jabuke ili pomorandže?
ROBERT:	Sok od jabuke onda . . . kako se kaže "ice," Jelena?
STJUARDESA:	Sa ledom?
ROBERT:	Bez leda, molim vas.
MARKO:	A za mene jednu flašu piva.
STJUARDESA:	Kafa, sok i pivo, izvolite.
SVI:	Hvala!
STJUARDESA:	Molim. Prijatno.

Terms of Politeness – Service

STEWARDESS:	Good afternoon. How are you?
ALL:	Good afternoon. (Very) well, thank you.
STEWARDESS:	Would you like a drink?
MARKO:	Who wants a drink? Jelena? Robert?
JELENA and ROBERT:	Yes, (please)!
STEWARDESS:	Please, what would you like?
MARKO:	Jelena, what would you like?
JELENA:	A coffee for me, please.
STEWARDESS:	White or black?
JELENA:	White, no sugar.
MARKO:	And you, Robert? Would you like (do you want) a beer?
ROBERT:	No, thanks. Excuse me, what else (more) do you have?
STEWARDESS:	Tea, fruit juice . . .
ROBERT:	A pineapple juice, please.
STEWARDESS:	I am sorry, but we have no pineapple juice. Apple juice or orange juice?
ROBERT:	Apple juice, then . . . how do you say "ice," Jelena?
STEWARDESS:	With ice?
ROBERT:	Without ice, please.
MARKO:	And for me, a bottle of beer.
STEWARDESS:	Coffee, juice, and beer, here you are.
ALL:	Thank you!
STEWARDESS:	You are welcome. Enjoy your drink.

VOCABULARY

beli,-a,-o	white
bez	without
bez leda	without ice
crni,-a,-o	black
čaj	tea
da	yes
da (with a verb)	to
flaša	bottle
hteti	to want
i	and
ili	or
izvolite	please (offering), here you are
jedan,-a,-o	one
još	more
kafa	coffee
kako se kaže . . .	how do you say . . .
led	ice
molim	please (asking)
ne	no
onda	then
piti	to drink
pivo	beer
prijatan,-na,-no	pleasant
sa ledom	with ice
sok od ananasa	pineapple juice
(sok od jabuke)	(apple juice)
(sok od pomorandže)	(orange juice)
šećer	sugar
voćni sok	fruit juice
za mene	for me

EXPLANATIONS

Greetings

The expression *dobar dan* (good day) is a formal greeting, used during most of the day.

Other greetings include:

Dobro jutro Good morning (used on arrival until about 10–11 A.M.)

Dobro veče Good evening (used on arrival from about 6–7 P.M.)

Dovidjenja Good-bye (used on departure, at any time)

Zbogom Good-bye (formal, used on departure)

Laku noć Good night (used on departure, late at night)

Prijatno* lit.: (Have a) pleasant (time) (friendly, used on departure)

Zdravo Hello (an informal greeting, used at any time)

Ćao Italian *ciao* (very informal, used any time, on arrival and departure)

*Prijatno is also used as an equivalent to the French *bon appétit* "enjoy your meal." (In this context in Croatian, the term *dobar tek* is used instead.)

Dobrodošli (welcome) is an expression used exclusively when greeting someone who has arrived somewhere for the first time (see Lesson One). It is not used in response to "thank you," as it is in English.

Terms of politeness

Molim has several meanings: "please," "I beg your pardon," and "you are welcome." *Molim* is also used when answering someone who has addressed you and, often, when answering the phone. *Molim* meaning "please" is not used as often as in English.

Izvolite is used when offering some service or an object. Therefore, *izvolite* can mean both "how can I help you?" and "here you are." People working in public service may answer the phone saying *izvolite*. The informal version of this term, used in singular form between friends, is *izvoli*; if several friends are addressed at the same time, the form *izvolite* or its shorter version *izvol'te* is used.

Hvala means "thank you" and is not used as often as in English. Various versions of saying "thank you" include:

Hvala lepo Thank you very much (lit.: thank you nicely)
Hvala puno or *Puno hvala* Thanks a lot; many thanks
Mnogo Vam hvala Thank you very much (has more emphasis)
Veliko hvala Big thanks

Nema na čemu is sometimes used instead of *molim* in response to "thank you" and signifies "not at all," "don't mention it." In informal situations *ništa* (lit.: nothing) also is used in response to "thank you" or in response to "I am sorry."

Izvinite is used both to attract someone's attention as in "excuse me" and as a mild apology as in "I am sorry." The informal version used in singular between friends is *izvini*. When addressing several friends at the same time the form *izvinite* is used. Sometimes it is used in combination with "please" for more emphasis—*Izvinite, molim Vas*; or informally—*Izvini, molim te.*

Žao mi je is a closer equivalent of the English "I am sorry." It is used to express apology or sympathy. A stronger version is *vrlo mi je žao* or *jako mi je žao* (I am very sorry).

EXAMPLE:

Gost: Izvinite? Konobar!?	Guest: Excuse me? Waiter!?
Konobar: Molim? (Izvolite?)	Waiter: Yes? (How can I help?)
Gost: Jedan sok od jabuke, molim.	Guest: One apple juice, please.

Konobar: Molim? (Izvinite?)	Waiter: Pardon? (Sorry?)
Gost: Jedan sok od jabuke!	Guest: One apple juice!
Konobar: Žao mi je, nemamo.	Waiter: I am sorry, we haven't got any.
Gost: Onda jedno pivo.	Guest: Then, a beer.
Konobar: Izvolite.	Waiter: Here you are.
Gost: Hvala lepo.	Guest: Thank you very much.
Konobar: Molim lepo.	Waiter: You are very welcome.

How are you?

Kako ste is a formal, polite version of "how are you?" It is also used among friends when addressing several people at the same time. The informal version, used in singular between friends, is *kako si?*

Sometimes the phrase *kako ste* is used in conjunction with *šta radite?*: *Kako ste? Šta radite?*—lit.: "How are you? What are you doing?" or "How are you doing?"

Possible answers to *kako ste* include:

Dobro, hvala. lit.: (I'm) well, thank you.
Hvala, a vi? Thanks, and you?
Nisam loše (hvala, a vi?) Not bad (thank you, and you?)
Vrlo dobro. Very well.
Nisam dobro. I'm not well.

Making an offer

There are various ways of making an offer. Some of these have been given in the dialogue above.

Želite li piće? Would you like a drink?

More assertive ways of inviting someone for a drink include:

Šta želite da popijete? What would you like to drink?

Šta pijete? What are you drinking?
Hoćete li jedno pivo? Would you like a beer?

"Yes" and "No"

For the most part, the affirmative *da* (yes) and the negative *ne* (no) are used as in the English language. *Da* is sometimes used when answering the phone.

N.B. The affirmative *da* meaning "yes" is not to be confused with the copula *da* as in: *Šta želite da popijete?* The copula *da* is used in complex sentences, similar to the English use of *to* with verbs (e.g.: What would you like to drink?).

GRAMMAR

Interrogative pronouns *ko* "who," *šta* "what," *kako* "how"

- The interrogative pronoun *ko* (*tko* in Croatian) is used to form questions referring to a person.

  Ko je ovo? Who is this?
  Ko želi piće? Who wants a drink?

- The interrogative pronoun *šta* (*što* in Croatian) is used to form questions referring to an object.

  Šta pijete? What are you drinking?
  Šta radite? What are you doing? (What do you do?)

- The interrogative pronoun *kako* is used to form a question of description or to determine more precise information.

  Kako ste? How are you?
  Kako se zovete? What are you called? (What is your name?)
  or
  Kako je vaše ime? What is your name?
  Kako se kaže . . .? How do you say . . .? (lit.: How is it said . . .?)

Declension of noun and adjectives

As noted in Lesson One, nouns and adjectives have seven cases in the singular and plural forms. The change of nouns and adjectives through each case is called declension. Here we shall explore four cases in the singular form on the basis of the examples given in the dialogue above. The plural forms of these cases as well as the other three cases in the singular and plural will be presented in the following three lessons.

The first case: Nominative (singular)

The nominative case answers the question: who / what? and is used to indicate the subject of the verb. The nominative form of nouns and adjectives is the one given in dictionaries.

sok juice; *kafa* coffee; *pivo* beer
dobar,-a,-o good; *hladan,-a,-o* cold

The second case: Genitive (singular)

The genitive case answers the question: from / of whom, from / of what? The genitive is used to indicate origin or to denote quantity (see examples below):

Masculine nouns acquire the ending *-a* in the genitive:

Čaša soka. A glass of juice.
Sok od ananasa. Pineapple juice (juice made of pineapple).

Feminine nouns lose the nominative ending *-a* and acquire the ending *-e*:

Šolja kafe. A cup of coffee.
Kolač od kafe. Coffeecake (a cake made of coffee).

Neuter nouns lose the ending *-o* and acquire the ending *-a*:

Flaša piva. A bottle of beer.
Mrlja od piva. A beer stain (a stain made from beer).

The genitive case can also be preceded by the preposition *bez* (without):

Kafa bez šećera. A coffee without sugar.
Sok bez leda. A (fruit) juice without ice.

The fourth case: Accusative (singular)

The accusative answers the question: who / what (do I see)? The accusative form of the noun is used when this noun is the direct object of the verb. After verbs such as *hteti* (to want), *imati* (to have), *nemati* (to not have), *piti* (to drink), and *želeti* (to wish), an accusative noun is usually required.

The noun *sok* (juice) is masculine singular, and its accusative form stays the same as in the nominative case:

Pijem sok. I am drinking a (fruit) juice.

The noun *kafa* (coffee), being of feminine gender, takes the form *kafu*:

*A ja pijem kaf*u̲. And I am drinking coffee.

The singular noun *pivo*, of neuter gender, stays the same in the accusative:

Ja pijem pivo. I am drinking beer.

When nouns are accompanied by adjectives, the case of the adjective corresponds with the case of the noun:

Pijem hladan sok. I am drinking a cold juice.
Pijem hladno pivo. I am drinking a cold beer.
Pijem hladnu kafu. I am drinking a cold coffee.

The nouns *sok*, *pivo*, and *kafa* are inanimate nouns. The accusative form of animate, masculine nouns acquires the ending -*a* (and the accompanying adjective acquires the ending -*og*):

*Imam (dobr*o̲*g) lekar*a̲. I have a (good) physician.

Animate nouns of other genders (feminine or neuter) have the same endings in the accusative as the inanimate nouns:

*Imam dobr*u̲ *profesork*u̲. I have a good (female) professor.
*Imam dobr*o̲ *det*e̲. I have a good child.

Accusative case of the number "one"

Jedan (one) differs from other numbers in that it can function as an adjective. As such it is often used like the indefinite article "a" (or "an") in English. As an adjective, *jedan* corresponds with the case, gender, and number of the noun that it accompanies.

Ja ću jedan sok. I'll (have) a juice. (masc./sing.)
A ja ću jedno pivo. And I'll (have) a beer. (neut./sing.)

In the accusative case, *jedna kafa* becomes:

Jednu kafu za mene, molim. A coffee for me, please. (fem./sing.)

The accusative form of the number "one" for animate objects of masculine gender is *jednog*:

Vidim jednog konobara. I (can) see a waiter.

Notice the "fleeting a" in *jedan* (as well as above in *hladan* "cold").

The sixth case: Instrumental (singular)

The sixth case, the instrumental, answers the questions: with whom / with what?

The masculine noun *šećer* (sugar) and the neuter noun *pivo* (beer) simply take the ending *-om*:

Kafa sa šećerom. A coffee with sugar.
Kolač sa pivom. A cake with beer.

Feminine nouns lose the nominative ending *-a* and also acquire the ending *-om*:

Kolač sa kafom. A cake with coffee.

The instrumental can be used to indicate an ingredient or an addition as in the examples above. It is also used to indicate company:

Marko putuje sa Jelenom i Robertom. Marko is traveling with Jelena and
Robert.

Or to indicate an instrument, a means, or a tool:

Marko putuje avionom. Marko is traveling by plane.

Please note that when referring to an instrument, a means, or a tool, the
instrumental is not accompanied by the preposition *sa* (with) or any other
preposition.

To sum up cases

EXAMPLES:

cases	*masc.*		*fem.*	*neut.*
1. Nominative – who / what?	sok	lekar	kafa	pivo
2. Genitive – of whom / what?	soka	lekara	kafe	piva
4. Accusative – whom / what?	sok	lekara	kafu	pivo
6. Instrumental – with whom / what?	sokom	lekarom	kafom	pivom

Present tense of *hteti* "to want"

Hteti (*htjeti* in *ijekavica*) is an irregular verb that does not fall into one of
the six classes of verbs. It is one of only two verbs in Serbo-Croat that ends
with *-u* in the first-person singular of the present tense. It also ends atypi-
cally with *-e* in both the third-person singular and plural forms. *Hteti* is both
a principal and an auxiliary verb. In its auxiliary mode, used to form the
future tense, it has a shortened version. (The future tense is presented in
Lesson Three.)

singular	*plural*
hoću (I want)	hoćemo (we want)
hoćeš (you want)	hoćete (you want)
hoće (he/she/it wants)	hoće (they want)

The short present tense version of *hteti*:

singular	*plural*
ću	ćemo
ćeš	ćete
će	će

The negative

The negative form of most verbs is created by placing the word *ne* in front of the verb, as in *ne raditi* (to not work).

Ne radim. I don't work.

Negative form of *hteti* "to want"

The negative form of the verb *hteti* is *ne hteti* (to not want). The negative present tense form, however, is built by adding the word *ne* as a prefix to the short present tense forms of *hteti*:

neću (I don't want)	nećemo (we don't want)
nećeš (you don't want)	nećete (you don't want)
neće (he/she/it doesn't want)	neće (they don't want)

This is one of the few cases in Serbo-Croat where the word *ne* is fused with the affirmative form to make the negative form.

Present tense of *imati* "to have"

The verb *imati* (to have) falls into the fifth class of verbs, ending with -*a* in the third-person singular and -*ju* in the third-person plural present tense forms.

imam (I have)	imamo (we have)
imaš (you have)	imate (you have)
ima (he/she/it has)	imaju (they have)

Negative form of *imati* "to have"

The negative form of *imati* is *nemati*. This is another of the few cases in Serbo-Croat where the word *ne* is fused with the affirmative form to make the negative form.

nemam (I do not have)   nemamo (we do not have)
nemaš (you do not have)   nemate (you do not have)
nema (he/she/it does not have)   nemaju (they do not have)

Nisam: The negative form of *jesam* "I am"

Nisam (I am not) is the third instance where the word *ne* has fused with the affirmative form to make up the negative form, here of "I am."

nisam (I am not)   nismo (we are not)
nisi (you are not)   niste (you are not)
nije (he/she/it is not)   nisu (they are not)

Present tense of *piti* "to drink"

The verb *piti* (to drink) is a fourth-class verb. Its infinitive stem (derived by dropping the ending *-ti*) ends in the vowel *i*. The present tense endings of the fourth-class verbs are: *-jem, -ješ, -je, -jemo, -jete, -ju*:

pijem (I drink)   pijemo (we drink)
piješ (you drink)   pijete (you drink)
pije (he/she/it drinks)   piju (they drink)

Present tense of *želeti* "to wish"

Želeti (to wish, to want) is a sixth-class verb like *raditi* and *govoriti* (see Lesson One).

želim (I wish, want)   želimo (we wish, want)
želiš (you wish, want)   želite (you wish, want)
želi (he/she/it wishes, wants)   žele (they wish, want)

USEFUL PHRASES

Dobar dan. Kako ste?
(dobbar-DAAN. KAKko-steh)
Good afternoon. How are you?

Ja sam dobro, hvala. A vi?
(YAH-sam DOBbroh, khvalah. ah-VIH)
I am well, thank you. And you?

Izvinite, kako se zovete?
(izVEEnitteh, KAKko-seh ZOVvetteh)
Excuse me, what is your name?

Šta želite da pijete?
(shtah-ZHELlitteh dah-PIYyetteh)
What would you like to drink?

Jednu belu kafu bez šećera, molim.
(YEDdnu BEHlu kaafu bez-SHEHcherrah, MOLlim)
One white coffee without sugar, please.

Jedno hladno pivo za mene, molim.
(YEDdnoh KHLAADdnoh PEEvoh za-MENneh, MOLlim)
One cold beer for me, please.

Šta imate od pića?
(shtah-IMmatteh od PEEchah)
What drinks do you have?

Imate li sok od jabuke?
(IMmatteh-lih sok-od-YABbookeh)
Do you have apple juice?

Sa ledom ili bez leda?
(sah-LEDdom ili bez-LEDdah)
With ice or without ice?

Kako se kaže . . .?
(KAKkoh-seh KAAzheh)
How do you say . . .?

EXERCISES

I. Answer the questions.

> e.g.: Je li Marko Amerikanac? Da, Marko je Amerikanac.
> Hoće li Marko jedan sok? Ne, Marko hoće jedno pivo.

1. Je li Jelena Amerikanka?
2. Je li Jelena profesor?
3. Govori li Marko srpskohrvatski?
4. Ide li Marko za Beograd?
5. Idu li Robert i Jelena na more?
6. Hoće li Robert pivo?
7. Želi li Jelena crnu kafu?
8. Želi li Robert sok sa ledom?

II. Answer the questions.

> e.g.: Šta Robert radi? Robert je profesor.
> Ko hoće jedno pivo? Marko hoće jedno pivo.

1. Šta Jelena radi?
2. Šta Marko radi?
3. Ko je profesor?
4. Ko je Francuz?
5. Šta Jelena želi da pije?
6. Ko hoće sok?
7. Ko govori srpskohrvatski? (Robert, Jelena i Marko . . .)

III. Translate into Serbo-Croat.

1. Good afternoon, how are you?
2. What is your name?
3. Robert is not a Yugoslav.
4. Jelena wants a white coffee without sugar.
5. Marko wishes a beer.
6. Robert drinks juice without ice.

7. The stewardess doesn't have orange juice.
8. What would you like to drink?
9. Who speaks English?
10. Do you have coffee?
11. Do you drink beer?

LESSON
THREE

DIALOGUE

Mesto – Cilj kretanja i lokacija

JELENA: Vi idete pravo na more?

MARKO: Ne, nemam direktan let. Ostaću u Beogradu jednu noć.

JELENA: Imate li nekoga u Beogradu?

MARKO: Moja rodbina je u Podgorici i u Sarajevu. Imam nekoliko prijatelja u Beogradu, ali ću odsesti u hotelu.

JELENA: Odakle su vaši roditelji?

MARKO: Tata je iz Crne Gore, a mama iz Srbije.

JELENA: A gde idete na more?

MARKO: U Budvu.

JELENA: Budva je lepa.

Place – Destination and Location

JELENA: You are going straight to the seaside?

MARKO: No, I don't have a direct flight. I'll stay in Belgrade for a night.

JELENA: Do you have (know) anyone in Belgrade?

MARKO: My relatives are in Podgorica and Sarajevo. I have several friends in Belgrade but I'll stay in a hotel.

JELENA: Where are your parents from?

MARKO: Dad is from Montenegro, and mom from Serbia.

JELENA: Whereabouts are you going at the seaside?

MARKO: To Budva.

JELENA: Budva is nice.

VOCABULARY

Crna Gora	Montenegro
direktan,-na,-no	direct
gde	where
hotel	hotel
iz	from
let	flight
mama	mom
neko	somebody
nekoliko	several
noć	night
odakle	from where
odsesti	to stay
pravo	straight, straightaway
prijatelj	friend
rodbina	relatives
tata	dad

GRAMMAR

Interrogative pronouns *gde* "where" and *odakle* "where from"

- The interrogative pronoun *gde* (where) is used to form questions referring to a particular place or location:

Gde je Budva? Where is Budva?
Gde idete na more? Where (exactly) at the seaside are you going?

Gde should be distinguished from the interrogative pronoun *kuda* that also means "where." The interrogative pronoun *kuda* refers to the destination of movement rather than a location, and therefore is more often used with the verb *ići* (to go):

Kuda idete? Where are you going?

- The interrogative pronoun *odakle* (where from) is used to form questions regarding place of origin:

Odakle ste? Where are you from?
Odakle su vaši roditelji? Where are your parents from?

Odakle translates as "where from" and does not require any additional prepositions. In response to a question regarding origin, however, the preposition *iz* (from) is used, followed by the place of origin in the genitive case:

Ja sam iz Beograda. I am from Belgrade.

Indefinite pronouns *neko* "someone" and *nešto* "something"

* *Neko* is an indefinite pronoun used:

1) when referring generally to someone unknown:

Imate li nekoga u Beogradu? Do you have anyone in Belgrade?

(Here *neko* is in the accusative singular form. The declension of pronouns will be discussed in Lessons Six and Seven. The declension of *neko* and *nešto* is the same as the declension of the interrogative pronouns *ko* and *šta* given in Lesson Six.)

2) when referring specifically to someone unknown:

Neko je na vratima. Someone is at the door. (There's someone at the door.)

3) when addressing any one of the people present:

Da li neko želi piće? Does anyone want a drink?

* The indefinite pronoun *nešto* is used similarly when referring to inanimate objects or nouns:

Želite li nešto da pijete? Do you want something to drink?

The plural of the possessive adjective *moj* "my"

As discussed in Lesson One, the possessive adjective *moj* (my) corresponds with the gender, case, and number of the noun it accompanies. Its nominative singular and plural forms are:

singular	*plural*
moj suprug (my husband)	moji prijatelji (my friends-masc.)
moja supruga (my wife)	moje prijateljice (my friends-fem.)
moje dete (my child)	moja deca (my children-neut.)

N.B. The noun *dete* (child) has no regular plural form. The collective noun *deca* is used instead. *Deca* is declined as a singular feminine noun.

Noun classes

We have seen so far that various nouns, depending on their gender and their nominative singular endings, take different case endings in each declension. Nouns can be divided into three classes on these grounds:

<u>CLASS 1</u>

* masculine and neuter nouns ending in a consonant or the vowels *o* or *e*:

  sok; *Marko*; *pivo*; *more*

* neuter nouns ending in -*e* that have an extended stem in some cases:

  dete (gen./sing.: dete-t-a); *vreme* (gen./sing.: vreme-n-a)

<u>CLASS 2</u>

* feminine nouns ending in -*a*:

  kafa; *prijateljica*; *Jelena*

* masculine nouns ending in -*a*:

  Nikola (Nicholas); *tata* (daddy)

<u>CLASS 3</u>

* feminine nouns ending in a consonant or in -*o*:

  noć (night); *stvar* (thing); *ljubav* (love); *so* (salt)

N.B. In declensions the majority of third-class nouns end in -*i*. The third-class noun *noć* is presented in Lesson Four.

Collective nouns

Collective nouns are singular in number and form but apply to more than one person or object. Collective nouns are therefore declined in the singular but imply plural. They do not always have a plural form.

For example, *rodbina* is a feminine collective noun. It means "a group of relatives." The noun referring to "a relative" is *rodjak*, which has its own plural form *rodjaci* (also meaning "relatives" but used in a more particular sense).

Although *rodbina* can have a grammatical plural like all other feminine nouns, its plural form is not commonly used. Therefore it is correct to say:

Moja rodbina je u Jugoslaviji. My relatives are in Yugoslavia.

Here the accompanying verb is in the third-person singular.

Some masculine collective nouns include: *narod* meaning "people" or "nation," *prtljag* (luggage), etc.

Neuter collective nouns include: *voće* (fruit), *lišće* (leaves), etc.

N.B. This may explain why some foreigners make the mistake in English of saying "people is . . ." rather than "people are . . ." since in some languages the noun "people" may be a collective noun used in the singular. In Serbo-Croat both the collective noun *narod* and the irregular plural of the noun *čovek* (man)—*ljudi* (men) are used to mean "people."

The first case: Nominative (plural)

Masculine nouns often take the ending *-i* in the nominative plural:

profesori (professors); *prijatelji* (friends)

Some monosyllabic masculine nouns acquire the ending -*ovi*:

sokovi (juices); *drugovi* (friends)

Feminine nouns normally lose the singular ending -*a* and acquire the ending -*e*:

prijateljice (friends); *kafe* (coffees)

Neuter nouns lose the ending -*o* or -*e* and acquire the ending -*a*:

sela (villages); *mora* (seas)

N.B. The masculine plural *prijatelji* (friends) can refer to masculine or mixed gender; the feminine plural *prijateljice* refers only to feminine gender.

The second case: Genitive (plural)

Masculine nouns acquire the ending -*a* in the genitive plural:

Imam nekoliko prijatelja u Beogradu. I have several (of my) friends in Belgrade.

Some monosyllabic masculine nouns acquire the ending -*ova* in the genitive plural, e.g. *sokova*.

Feminine and neuter nouns take the ending -*a* in the genitive plural:

prijateljica; *kafa*

sela; *mora*

N.B. In pronunciation, the penultimate syllable of the word in the genitive case acquires a stress and the stressed vowel is long. Therefore the genitive stress of the nominative PRIyately moves to priyaTELYa, and the "e" is long. Similarly, the short "e" in SELla remains stressed but becomes longer: SEYla.

The fourth case: Accusative (plural)

Masculine nouns acquire the ending -e in the accusative plural:

Imam prijatelje u Beogradu. I have friends in Belgrade.

Feminine nouns also take the ending -e. The accusative plural form of feminine nouns is therefore equivalent to the nominative plural form: *prijateljice.*

Neuter nouns take the ending -a instead of the endings -o or -e, their accusative plural being equivalent to their nominative plural: *sela, mora.*

The sixth case: Instrumental (plural)

Masculine nouns acquire the ending -ima in the instrumental plural:

Putujem sa prijateljima. I am traveling with friends.

Feminine nouns acquire the ending -ma in the instrumental plural:

Putujem sa prijateljicama. I am traveling with (female) friends.

Neuter nouns drop the ending -e or -o and acquire the ending -ima:

morima (with the seas); *selima* (with the villages)

The seventh case: Prepositional (singular and plural)

The seventh case, the prepositional (also called "locative"), is used to determine the location of something or someone and answers the questions "where?" (*gde*) and "in / on / about whom / what?" It is most often accompanied by the prepositions *u* (in) and *na* (on).

The prepositional is often used with the names of places. *Beograd* is a masculine noun. Its prepositional form is *Beogradu.*

Imam prijatelje u Beogradu. I have friends in Belgrade.

The noun *Podgorica* (the capital of Montenegro) is feminine. Its nominative ending *-a* is replaced by the ending *-i*:

Imam prijatelje u Podgorici. I have friends in Podgorica.

The noun *Sarajevo* (the capital of Bosnia) is neuter. Its form in the prepositional is the same as for masculine nouns. The final vocal *-o* is replaced by the prepositional ending *-u* for masculine and neuter nouns:

Imam prijatelje u Sarajevu. I have friends in Sarajevo.

It is important to distinguish the prepositional from the accusative; a noun in the accusative case can be accompanied by similar prepositions and can also refer to a place. The accusative forms of the names of these cities are presented here:

Idem u Beograd. I am going to Belgrade.
Idem u Podgoricu. I am going to Podgorica.
Idem u Sarajevo. I am going to Sarajevo.

While the accusative indicates destination of movement, the prepositional indicates location—where the object or person in question is situated.

In the plural the prepositional has the same endings as the instrumental plural (*-ima* for masculine and neuter nouns and *-ma* for the feminine nouns). The notable difference between the prepositional and the instrumental is that the prepositional is accompanied by the locative prepositions *na* (on), *u* (in), and *o* (about) rather than *sa* "with."

Present tense of *ostati* "to stay"

Ostati belongs to the third class of verbs. The third-class verbs take the endings *-em*, *-eš*, *-e*, *-emo*, *-ete*, *-u* in the present tense. The verb *ostati*, however, takes an additional *-n-* between the infinitive stem and the present tense endings. This is because most other third-class verbs have the infinitive stem ending -*nu*, whereas the verb *ostati* does not. Therefore:

singular	*plural*
ostanem (I stay)	ostanemo (we stay)
ostaneš (you stay)	ostanete (you stay)
ostane (he/she/it stays)	ostanu (they stay)

Ostati is a perfective verb. This means that it most commonly appears as a secondary verb accompanied by the copula *da*, in a present tense sentence.

Želim __da__ ostanem u Beogradu. I wish to stay in Belgrade.

N.B. Please see the following lesson for more on perfective and imperfective verbs.

Odsesti "to stay"

The verb *odsesti* also translates as "to stay." Unlike the verb *ostati* that denotes the action of staying or staying behind, *odsesti* relates more specifically to accommodations. It is most commonly used in conjunction with a form of accommodation (in the prepositional):

Želim da odsednem u hotelu. I'd like to stay in a hotel.

Odsesti is derived from the verb *sesti* (to sit), which belongs to the first class of verbs. Note that the first-class verbs have the greatest number of variations and inconsistent rules. The verbs *sesti* and *odsesti* are discussed additionally in Lesson Five.

Present tense of *odsesti* (to stay):

odsednem	odsednemo
odsedneš	odsednete
odsedne	odsednu

N.B. *Odsesti*, like *ostati*, is a perfective verb that requires the copula *da*, and often accompanies another, primary verb in the present tense.

Želim da odsednem u hotelu "Hilton." I wish to stay at the Hilton hotel.

The future tense

The affirmative form of the future tense is built using the infinitive of a verb and the short present tense forms of the auxiliary verb *hteti*:

ja ću ostati (I will stay)	mi ćemo ostati (you will stay)
ti ćeš ostati (you will stay)	vi ćete ostati (we will stay)
on/ona/ono će ostati (he/she/it will stay)	oni/one/ona će ostati (they will stay)

A shorter version of the future tense is built by adding the short present tense form of *hteti* to the infinitive stem of the verb. The infinitive stem is derived by dropping the infinitive ending *-ti* (*ostati* minus the infinitive ending *-ti* gives the infinitive stem *osta-*).

ostaću (I'll stay)	ostaćemo (we'll stay)
ostaćeš (you'll stay)	ostaćete (you'll stay)
ostaće (he/she/it'll stay)	ostaće (they'll stay)

This short version of the future tense is always used without a pronoun; the long version is always used with a pronoun. The long form tends to be used when the emphasis is on the subject (e.g. *Ja ću ostati u Beogradu, a on će ostati u Njujorku.* "I will stay in Belgrade and he will stay in New York").

In this example, *ostati* (to stay) is followed by the location in the prepositional case:

Ostaću u Beogradu. I'll stay in Belgrade.

If the duration of the stay is specified, the location is in the accusative case:

Ostaću u Beogradu jedan dan. I'll stay in Belgrade one day.
Ostaću u Beogradu jednu noć. * I'll stay in Belgrade one night.

*Noć is one of the rare feminine nouns ending in a consonant (see Lesson Four). The accompanying adjectival number one agrees with *noć* in feminine gender.

USEFUL PHRASES

Odakle ste?
(odDAKleh steh)
Where are you from?

Ja sam iz Kalifornije.
(YAH-sam iz-kaliFORniyeh)
I am from California.

Gde idete?
(gdeh-IDetteh)
Where are you going?

Idem na more.
(IDdem nah MORreh)
I am going to the seaside.

Ostaću u Beogradu jednu noć.
(OSStachu u-behOHGgradu YEDdnu nohoch)
I'll stay in Belgrade one night.

Odsešću u hotelu.
(ODSseshchu u-hoTELloo)
I'll stay in a hotel.

Imam rodbinu u Jugoslaviji.
(IMMam RODbinnu u-yuGOSslaviyih)
I have relatives in Yugoslavia.

Imam nekoliko prijatelja u Beogradu.
(IMMam NEKkoliko priyaTELYah u-behOGgradu)
I have several friends in Belgrade.

EXERCISES

I. Answer the questions.

e.g.: Odakle je Marko?
   Marko je iz Amerike.

1. Gde Marko ide?
2. Gde Robert ide?
3. Odakle je Jelena?
4. Ima li Marko direktan let za more?
5. Gde će Marko odsesti?

II. Put the words in parentheses into the appropriate forms.

e.g.: Marko: Moja rodbina (biti) u (Podgorica) i u (Sarajevo).
   Marko: Moja rodbina je u Podgorici i u Sarajevu.

1. Marko (ići) u (Budva).
2. Moji roditelji (biti) iz (Amerika).
3. Marko (imati) nekoliko (prijatelj) u (Beograd).
4. Ja (imati) (rodbina) u (Kanada) i u (Meksiko).*
5. Ja (želeti) (ostati) u (Beograd).
6. Ja (želeti) (odsesti) u (hotel) (jedan) (noć).

Kanada (Canada) is declined as a feminine noun, and *Meksiko* (Mexico) as a neuter noun.

III. Decline the following nouns in all of the cases that you know (nominative singular and plural, genitive singular and plural, accusative singular and plural, instrumental singular and plural, and prepositional singular and plural).

hotel (masc.)
tata (masc.)
mama (fem.)

LESSON FOUR

DIALOGUE

Vreme

ROBERT: Koliko ostajete na moru?

MARKO: Deset dana na moru i nedelju dana u Podgorici. A koliko ostajete u Beogradu?

ROBERT: Jelena ostaje mesec dana, a ja dve nedelje.

JELENA: Izvinite, da li neko zna koliko ima sati?

MARKO: Dva i deset. Ali moj sat žuri nekoliko minuta.

ROBERT: A u koliko sati stižemo? U pola četiri?

JELENA: Da, ali malo kasnimo. Stići ćemo oko petnaest do četiri.

Time

ROBERT: How long are you staying at the seaside?

MARKO: Ten days at the seaside and a week in Podgorica. And how long are you staying in Belgrade?

ROBERT: Jelena is staying for a month, and I am staying for two weeks.

JELENA: Excuse me, does anyone know what time it is?

MARKO: Ten past two. But my watch is several minutes fast.

ROBERT: And at what time do we arrive? At half past three?

JELENA: Yes, but we are a little late. We'll arrive at around quarter to four.

VOCABULARY

četiri	four
dan	day
deset	ten
dva,-e,-a	two
(Croatian: dva, dvije, dva)	
kasniti	to be late
koliko	how much, how long
malo	a little
mesec	month
(Croatian: mjesec)	
nedelja	week
(Croatian: tjedan)	
nekoliko	several
oko	around
ostati	to stay
petnaest	fifteen
pola	half
sat (also: čas "hour")	hour; watch, clock
stići	to arrive
u	in
u koliko sati	at what time
znati	to know
žuriti	to be fast, to hurry

EXPLANATIONS

Numbers

0 - nula	15 - petnaest (*or* petnest)
1 - jedan	16 - šesnaest (*or* šesnest)
2 - dva	17 - sedamnaest (*or* sedamnest)
3 - tri	18 - osamnaest (*or* osamnest)
4 - četiri (or čet'ri)	19 - devetnaest (*or* devetnest)
5 - pet	20 - dvadeset
6 - šest	21 - dvadeset jedan
7 - sedam	25 - dvadeset pet
8 - osam	30 - trideset
9 - devet	35 - trideset pet
10 - deset	40 - četrdeset
11 - jedanaest (*or* jedanest)	45 - četrdeset pet
12 - dvanaest (*or* dvanest)	50 - pedeset
13 - trinaest (*or* trinest)	55 - pedeset pet
14 - četrnaest (*or* četrnest)	60 - šezdeset

Except for the number one, cardinal numbers, in general, do not have declensions. Numbers two, three, and four have grammatical declensions, but there are archaic and not widely used. Also, *nula* (zero) is fully declined as a feminine noun.

Time

There are several ways of asking for the time in Serbo-Croat:

Koliko ima sati? What's the time? (lit.: How many hours are there?)

Koliko je sati? What's the time? (lit.: How many hours is it?)

Ima li neko sat? Does anyone have the time? (lit.: Does anyone have a watch?)

Da li neko zna koliko ima sati? Does anyone know what time it is?

Usually a twelve-hour clock is used when giving the time. In very formal situations and in schedules a twenty-four-hour clock is used.

Time is normally given in this way:

jedan i pet five past one (lit.: one and five)
jedan i petnaest quarter past one (lit.: one and fifteen)
petnaest do dva quarter to two (lit.: fifteen to two)
pet do dva five to two, etc.

Important! *Pola dva* (lit.: half two) actually means "half past one." To avoid confusion, this can also be expressed as: *jedan i trideset* (lit.: one and thirty).

In some parts of Yugoslavia, such as Montenegro, the following format is used:

jedan i po lit.: one and a half (Croatian: *jedan i pol*)

Other temporal determiners

Other temporal determiners include:

ujutro or *ujutru** in the morning
prepodne before noon, A.M.
podne midday, noon
popodne or *posle podne** afternoon, P.M.
uveče in the evening
ponoć midnight
posle ponoći after midnight

*These are used interchangeably.

Therefore:
sedam ujutro = 7 A.M.
sedam uveče = 7 P.M.
dva popodne = 2 P.M.
dva ujutro or *dva posle ponoći* = 2 A.M.

Temporal adverbs

Adverbs are unchangeable—they do not have declensions—and are used to describe more closely other words. Most often they accompany verbs, but they can accompany adjectives, nouns, and other adverbs. Adverbs are discussed in more detail in Lesson Seven.

The above temporal determiners are actually temporal adverbs. Other temporal adverbs include:

prekjuče the day before yesterday
juče yesterday
sinoć last night
jutros this morning
danas today
večeras this evening
noćas tonight
sutra tomorrow
prekosutra or *preksutra* the day after tomorrow

GRAMMAR

Interrogative pronoun *koliko* "how much"

The interrogative pronoun *koliko* is used to make up questions referring to quantity.

Koliko je sati? lit.: How many hours is it? (What's the time?)

It can also refer to a length of time as in:

Koliko ostajete u Beogradu? How (much) long are you staying in Belgrade?

The interrogative pronoun *koliko* can have several meanings in English: "how many," "how much," and "how long."

Indefinite pronoun *nekoliko* "some" or "several"

The pronoun *nekoliko* is used to refer to an indefinite quantity:

Imam nekoliko prijatelja u Beogradu. I have some / several friends in Belgrade.

Moj sat žuri nekoliko minuta. My watch is several minutes fast.

Nouns accompanying numbers

Time can also be given in this way:

jedan sat i pet minuta five minutes past one (lit.: one o'clock and five minutes)

pet minuta do jedan (sat) lit.: five minutes to one (o'clock)

Nouns accompanying the number one are always in the nominative singular (unless "one" is used as an adjective, in which case it and the noun are inflected accordingly, as explained in Lesson Two). When counting or giving time, the number one and any accompanying noun appear in the nominative:

jedan sat i jedan minut one minute past one (lit.: one hour and one minute)

In contrast, masculine nouns accompanying numbers two, three, and four are in the genitive singular:

dva sata i tri minuta lit.: two hours and three minutes

Nouns accompanying other numbers take the genitive plural:

pet sati i deset minuta lit.: five hours and ten minutes

N.B. *Sat* is one of the rare masculine nouns that take different forms in the genitive singular and genitive plural (*sata, sati*).

Sat "hour"

Sat (pronounced with a long "a" as in "art") meaning "hour" is a masculine noun. Its nominative plural form is *sati*, its genitive singular is *sata*, and its genitive plural—*sati*. Therefore:

jedan sat, dva sata, tri sata . . .

But:

pet sati, deset sati, dvanaest sati . . .

The same applies with compound numbers, such as:

dvadeset jedan sat, dvadeset dva sata, dvadeset tri sata

But:

dvadeset pet sati, dvadest osam sati, trideset sati

Minut "minute"

Minut is also a masculine noun. Its genitive singular form is *minuti* and its genitive singular and genitive plural are the same—*minuta*.

jedan minut, dva minuta, pet minuta, dvadeset minuta

When accompanying compound numbers that include the number one, the noun is always in the nominative singular:

dvadeset jedan minut, trideset jedan minut

In Croatian the noun "minute" is of feminine gender: *minuta*. Feminine nouns take the nominative plural endings when accompanying numbers two, three, and four, and take the genitive plural endings when accompanying all other numbers. The nominative plural of "minute" is *minute* and its genitive plural is *minuta*.

In Croatian (notice the *ijekavica* version of feminine "two," *dvije*):

jedna minuta, dvije minute, pet minuta, dvadeset minuta
dvadeset jedna minuta, dvadeset dvije minute

case	*singular (masc.)*		*plural (masc.)*	
Nominative:	sat	minut	sati	minuti
Genitive:	sata	minuta	sati	minuta

case	*singular (fem.)*	*plural (fem.)*
Nominative:	minuta	minute
Genitive:	minute	minuta

Sat meaning "clock" or "watch"

Sat (also pronounced with a long "a") can mean also "clock" or "watch" (or in Croatian—"a school lesson"). The noun *sat* with this meaning has

different plural forms. Its nominative plural is *satovi* and its genitive plural—
satova. Therefore:

jedan sat, dva sata

But:

pet satova, deset satova . . .

Čas "hour"

The noun *čas* has several meanings one of which is "hour" (also in Serbian—
"a school lesson"). It is used in formal situations and more often in the plural
form. Its plural is similar to the plural of *sat* meaning "clock":

jedan čas one hour
dvanaest časova twelve hours
dvadeset četiri časa twenty-four hours

case	singular (masc.)		plural (masc.)	
Nominative:	sat	čas	satovi	časovi
Genitive:	sata	časa	satova	časova

Dan "day"

Dan is a masculine noun (pronounced with a long "a"):

case	singular (masc.)	plural (masc.)
Nominative:	dan	dani
Genitive:	dana	dana

Therefore:

jedan dan, dva dana, pet dana

Mesec "month"

Mesec (in *ijekavica: mjesec*) means "month." It is a masculine noun and is declined like the noun *sat* meaning "hour."

case	*singular (masc.)*	*plural (masc.)*
Nominative:	mesec	meseci
Genitive:	meseca	meseci
(Accusative:	mesec	mesece)

jedan mesec, dva meseca, pet meseci

Mesec is pronounced with an emphasis on the first syllable (MEHsets). In the plural form, however, the emphasis moves to the second syllable and the second "e" is long (mehSEYtsi).

In response to a question concerning duration (*Koliko* . . . "How long . . ."), it is possible to use either the expression *jedan mesec* (one month) or *mesec dana* (month of days) to indicate the number of days in question. In the expression *mesec dana*, the noun *mesec* is in the accusative case and the noun *dan* is in the genitive plural case (when used in response to a question). Note that is not possible to say *jedan mesec dana* or *dva meseca dana*, etc. The expression *mesec dana* is only used when referring to the duration of one month.

Mesec can also mean "moon." With this meaning, it is declined like other masculine nouns.

Nedelja "week"

Nedelja is a feminine noun:

case	*singular (fem.)*	*plural (fem.)*
Nominative:	nedelja	nedelje
Genitive:	nedelje	nedelja
(Accusative:	nedelju	nedelje)

Nedelja can also mean "Sunday." It is always declined in the same way. Its form in *ijekavica*, as spoken in Montenegro, is *nedjelja*. (In Croatian, the word for "week" is *tjedan*, and the word for "Sunday" is also *nedjelja*.)

In response to a question concerning duration, it is possible to use either the expression *jednu nedelju* (one week) or *nedelju dana* (week of days). *Jedan* (one) has to correspond with the feminine gender of the noun *nedelja*, therefore the nominative form is *jedna nedelja*. In the expression *jednu nedelju* both *jedan* and the noun *nedelja* are in the accusative singular. In the expression *nedelju dana* the noun *nedelja* is in the accusative singular and the noun *dan* is in the genitive plural. The expression *nedelju dana* is used only when referring to the duration of one week. It is not possible to say *dve nedelje dana*, etc. However, other possible answers include: *dve nedelje* (number two also corresponds with the feminine gender of the noun), *tri nedelje*, *pet nedelja*, etc. In these cases the number is in the accusative and the noun is either in the genitive singular or the genitive plural accordingly (see rules above on nouns accompanying numbers).

Noć "night"

Noć is one of the rare feminine nouns that end in a consonant. These nouns are declined slightly differently than other feminine nouns:

case	singular (fem.)	plural (masc.)
Nominative:	noć	noći
Genitive:	noći	noći
(Accusative:	noć	noći)

In response to a question concerning duration, the answer may be *jednu noć*, *dve noći*, *pet noći*, etc. Numbers *jedan* (one) and *dva* (two) correspond with the feminine gender of the noun *noć*. Therefore the nominative forms would be: *jedna noć* and *dve noći*. All other numbers (except compound numbers involving numbers one and two, such as: twenty-one, thirty-two, etc.) do not have to agree with the gender of the noun they accompany. In the expression *jednu noć*, both the number and the noun are in the accusative singular.

Summary of declensions

The singular forms of the number "one" accompanying a noun and the plural of the noun:

Masculine:
Monosyllabic, inanimate noun:

case	_singular_	_plural_
1. Nominative:	jedan sat	sati
2. Genitive:	jednog sata	sati
4. Accusative:	jedan sat	sate
6. Instrumental:	jednim* satom	satima
7. Prepositional:	jednom satu	satima

Polysyllabic, animate noun:

case	_singular_	_plural_
1. Nominative:	jedan prijatelj	prijatelji
2. Genitive:	jednog prijatelja	prijatelja
4. Accusative:	jednog prijatelja	prijatelje
6. Instrumental:	jednim prijateljem**	prijateljima
7. Prepositional:	jednom prijatelju	prijateljima

 *"One" takes the ending -*im* in the instrumental.
**The noun *prijatelj* takes the ending -*em* in the instrumental singular because of its soft ending "lj." See Lesson Five for more detail on the instrumental case.

Feminine:
Noun ending with a vowel:

case	_singular_	_plural_
1. Nominative:	jedna prijateljica	prijateljice
2. Genitive:	jedne prijateljice	prijateljica
4. Accusative:	jednu prijateljicu	prijateljice
6. Instrumental:	jednom prijateljicom	prijateljicama
7. Prepositional:	jednoj prijateljici	prijateljicama

Noun ending with a consonant:

case	singular	plural
1. Nominative:	jedna noć	noći
2. Genitive:	jedne noći	noći
4. Accusative:	jednu noć	noći
6. Instrumental:	jednom noći	noćima
7. Prepositional:	jednoj noći	noćima

Neuter nouns:

case	singular	plural
1. Nominative:	jedno more	mora
2. Genitive:	jednog mora	mora
4. Accusative:	jedno more	mora
6. Instrumental:	jednim morem	morima
7. Prepositional:	jednom moru	morima

Imperfective and perfective meaning of verbs

In all Slavonic languages including Serbo-Croat, verbs can have an imperfective or a perfective meaning, which is indicated by a particular form of that verb.

Verbs in the imperfective form indicate an action or a state of unlimited duration or habitual nature:

piti to drink; *ostajati* to stay; *kasniti* to be late

Verbs in the perfective form indicate either completion of an action or state, or an action or state that is limited in type and duration:

popiti to drink up; *ostati* to stay; *zakasniti* to be late

Perfective use

Šta želite da popijete? What would you like to drink?
Želim (da popijem) jednu kafu. I would like (to have/drink) a coffee.

Perfective verbs in the present tense often appear as secondary verbs in the sentence and are accompanied by the copula *da*. In the examples above, the primary verb is *želeti* (to wish), but other verbs can appear as primary verbs too, as perfective verbs can rarely stand on their own. In an informal register, it is possible for the perfective verb to appear as the only verb in an interrogative sentence, as illustrated in the final example. Here the primary verb *hteti* is implied.

(Hoćemo li) da popijemo po jednu kafu? (Shall we) have (drink) a coffee (each)?

The use of a primary verb in such a question is optional.

Imperfective use

Šta pijete? What are you drinking?

This indicates an offer, a habit, or an action that is already taking place. For example:

Šta radite? What are you doing?
Pijem. I am drinking.
Šta pijete? What are you drinking?
Pijem kafu. I am drinking coffee.

Similarly, *Želim da pijem kafu* (I'd like to drink coffee) is simply the expression of a desire, which may not necessarily imply a response to an immediate offer, and where the time and duration of the desired action is irrelevant.

N.B. Imperfective verbs more commonly appear as primary verbs in sentences (e.g. *Pijem kafu* "I am drinking coffee") while perfective verbs often appear as secondary verbs and are therefore preceded by the copula *da* (e.g.

Šta želite da popijete? "What would you like to drink?"where *želite* is a primary and *popijete* a secondary verb).

Also notice that imperfective and perfective verbs often appear in pairs, where a perfective verb is a derivation from its imperfective equivalent (e.g. imperfective *piti* and perfective *po-piti*; *kasniti* and *za-kasniti*, etc.).

Imperfective *ostajati* and perfective *ostati* "to stay"

singular	plural	singular	plural
ostajem	ostajemo	ostanem	ostanemo
ostaješ	ostajete	ostaneš	ostanete
ostaje	ostaju	ostane	ostanu

Koliko ostajete u Beogradu? How long are you staying in Belgrade?

In this question the present tense of the verb *ostajati* is used to indicate duration that may be unlimited.

The present tense of the verb *ostati*, however, does not indicate duration but completion of an action. Therefore:

Želim da ostanem u Beogradu. I want to stay in Belgrade.

This can mean: "I want to stay behind in Belgrade" or "I want to remain in Belgrade indefinitely."

N.B. *Ostati* is derived from *stati* (to stop).

The interrogative future tense

Since the imperfective *ostajati* is unlimited in duration, its use in the present tense can indicate the future in the same way that the present tense in English can indicate the future:

Koliko ostajete u Beogradu? How long are you staying / going to stay in Belgrade?

Another way of asking the same question is:

Koliko ćete ostati u Beogradu? How long will you stay in Belgrade?

In this example the infinitive of the perfective *ostati* is used with the short present tense form of the verb *hteti* to build the future tense:

Koliko ću ostati?	Koliko ćemo ostati?
Koliko ćeš ostati?	Koliko ćete ostati?
Koliko će ostati?	Koliko će ostati?

It is possible to build the future tense for any verb in this way regardless of whether it is imperfective or perfective. However, the future tense of imperfective verbs may indicate an action that will be repeating or occurring habitually in the future, while the future tense of perfective verbs indicates an action of limited duration that will occur. Hence, the future tense of the verb *ostajati* (*ostajaću, ostajaćeš, ostajaće,* etc.) indicates an action of a particular duration that will be repeating itself at regular intervals, whereas the future tense of the verb *ostati* (*ostaću, ostaćeš, ostaće,* etc.) indicates an action of limited duration that will occur in the future.

The negative future tense

The negative construction of the future tense is built by using the negative form of the verb *hteti-ne hteti* (as presented in Lesson Two) followed by the main verb in the infinitive:

Neću ostati u Beogradu. I won't stay in Belgrade.
Nećete ostati u Beogradu. You won't stay in Belgrade.

Question formation: The interrogative *da li*

In Lesson One we examined two ways of forming questions: 1) turning a statement into a question by changing intonation and 2) changing the word order by placing the verb followed by the interrogative particle *li* at the beginning of the sentence.

Another common way to form a question is with the question marker *da li*:

Da li neko zna koliko ima sati? Does anyone know what time it is?

Here the pattern is:

Da li + (subject) + verb + object (secondary sentence/phrase)

Da li + *neko* + *zna* + *koliko ima sati?*

Depending on context, the subject or pronoun can be left out—if it is made clear by the form of the verb. In the above example the subject is not specified. The use of the indeterminate pronoun *neko* implies that the question is addressed to anyone present.

Da li znate koliko ima sati? Do you know what time it is?
(*Da li* + inflected verb + secondary sentence)

In this example, the second-person form of the verb *znati* addresses a person or a number of people directly and therefore does not require a pronoun.

The question:

Da li vi znate koliko ima sati? Do you know what time it is?

is perfectly possible; but, formulated in this way (i.e. keeping the pronoun for emphasis), the question indicates that somebody else has already given a negative answer. For example:

A: *Da li znate koliko ima sati?*   A: Do you know what time it is?
B: *Žao mi je, ne znam.*   B: Sorry, I don't know.
A: *Da li vi znate koliko ima sati?* A: Do you know what time it is?
C: *Dva i deset.*   C: Ten past two.

Question formation with the question marker *da li* follows a slightly different pattern when using auxiliary verbs such as *hteti* and *jesam*—the present tense of the verb "to be":

Da li + auxiliary verb + (subject) + object (secondary sentence/phrase)

Da li sam ja Jugosloven? Am I a Yugoslav?
Da li ste srećni? Are you happy?
Da li ćemo ići na more? Will we go to the seaside?
Da li ćete ostati u Beogradu? Will you stay in Belgrade?

N.B. The question marker *da li* is always pronounced as one word in which both vowels are short. The stress in the sentence is almost never on the question marker.

USEFUL PHRASES

Koliko ostajete u Beogradu?
(kolLIKkoh OSstahyetteh u-behOGgradu)
How long are you staying in Belgrade?

Ostaću u Beogradu četiri dana i pet noći.
(OSstahchu u-behOGgradu CHETtirih DAANnah ih peiht NOHchih)
I'll stay in Belgrade for four days and five nights.

Moji prijatelji žele da ostanu u Jugoslaviji mesec dana.
(MOHyih priYATtelyih ZHEleh-dah OSstahnu u yuGOSslaviyih MESsetz
    DAANna)
My friends want to stay in Yugoslavia for a month.

Koliko ima sati?
(kolLIKko-IMmah SAATtih)
What's the time?

Da li znate koliko je sati?
(dah-lih ZNATteh kolLIKkoh-yeh SAATtih)
Do you know what time it is?

Sada je sedam sati i deset minuta.
(SADdah-yeh SEDdam SAATtih-ih-DESset minNOOtah)
Now it is ten past seven.

U koliko sati stižemo?
(u-kolLIKko SAATtih STIzhemmoh)
At what time do we arrive?

Kasnimo pola sata.
(KASsnimoh POLlah SAATtah)
We are (running) half an hour late.

Stižemo do pola devet.
(STIzhemmoh do POLlah-DEVvet)
We wll arrive by half past eight.

Stićićemo na vreme.
(STIchichemoh nah-VREMmeh)
We will arrive on time.

EXERCISES

I.   Answer the questions.

e.g.: Koliko Marko ostaje u Beogradu?
      Marko ostaje u Beogradu jednu noć.

1. Koliko Jelena ostaje u Beogradu?
2. A koliko Robert ostaje u Beogradu?
3. Koliko Marko ostaje na moru?
4. A u Podgorici?
5. Da li Marko ima nekoga u Beogradu?
6. Gde Marko ide na more?
7. U koliko sati stižu Marko, Jelena i Robert?
8. Da li oni kasne?
9. Koliko kasne?

II. Conjugate the following verbs in the present tense.

popiti (to drink up)
kasniti (to be late)
stati (to stop)

Then conjugate the same verbs in the future tense (in both the short and long forms).

III. Turn the statements into questions using three different patterns of question formation.

1. Robert ide na konferenciju u Beograd.
2. Marko ostaje u Beogradu jednu noć.
3. Marko ima prijatelje u Beogradu.
4. Avion kasni pola sata.
5. Marko, Jelena i Robert stižu u Beograd na vreme.

Turn the same statements into questions using the interrogative pronouns "who," "what," "how much/long," and "where."

e.g.: Marko ostaje u Podgorici nedelju dana.
    Ko ostaje u Podgorici nedelju dana?
    Koliko Marko ostaje u Podgorici?
    Gde Marko ostaje nedelju dana?

IV. Decline these nouns in each of the following cases (nominative, genitive, accusative, instrumental, and prepositional, in both singular and plural).

profesor
sok
kafa
stjuardesa
pivo
selo

LESSON
FIVE

DIALOGUE

Dogovori

MARKO: Gde vi odsedate?

ROBERT: Kod Jeleninih roditelja. A vi?

MARKO: Verovatno ću odsesti u hotelu "Slavija."

JELENA: Odlično, možemo vas odbaciti do hotela. I mi idemo prema Slaviji.

MARKO: A, ne, ne. Idem ja taksijem. Imam puno stvari.

ROBERT: Taksi na aerodromu je vrlo skup. Nas čeka Jelenin brat kolima-ima dovoljno prostora.

MARKO: Onda ćete mi dozvoliti da vas bar pozovem na piće večeras?

ROBERT: Dogovorićemo se.

JELENA: Ustvari možete se vi nama pridružiti na večeri. Mi idemo u Skadar-liju večeras. To je Robertovo omiljeno mesto u Beogradu.

MARKO: Nisam siguran . . .

ROBERT: Zašto da ne?

MARKO: Malo sam umoran.

JELENA: Onda ćete se prvo odmoriti. Imamo dovoljno vremena do večere.

MARKO: Dobro, onda. Možda vam se pridružim.

Making Arrangements

MARKO: Where are you staying?

ROBERT: At Jelena's parents. And you?

MARKO: I'll probably stay at the hotel "Slavija."

JELENA: Excellent. We can give you a lift to the hotel. We're going towards Slavija too.

MARKO: Oh, no, no. I'll go by taxi. I have a lot of things.

ROBERT: A taxi at the airport is very expensive. Jelena's brother will be waiting for us with a (by) car—there is enough space.

MARKO: Then you will allow me at least to invite you for a drink tonight.

ROBERT: We'll arrange something. (We'll talk about it.)

JELENA: In fact, you can join us for dinner. We are going to Skadarlija tonight. That's Robert's favorite place in Belgrade.

MARKO: I'm not sure . . .

ROBERT: Why not?

MARKO: I'm a little tired.

JELENA: Then you will (take a) rest first. We have enough time until dinner.

MARKO: OK, then. Maybe I'll join you.

VOCABULARY

aerodrom	airport
bar	at least
brat	brother
čekati	to wait
do	to
dobro	good, OK, all right
dogovor	arrangement
dogovoriti se	to agree, to make an arrangement
dovoljno	enough
dozvoliti	to allow
kola	car
malo	little
mesto	place
moći	to be able to
možda	maybe
možemo	we can
nisam siguran	I'm not sure
odbaciti	to give a lift, to give a ride
odlično	excellent
odmoriti se	to take a rest
omiljen,-a,-o	favorite
pozvati	to invite
pridružiti se	to join
prostor	space
prvo	first
puno	a lot
Skadarlija	an old-fashioned street in Belgrade, with restaurants
skup	expensive
Slavija	a hotel in Belgrade, also a district in central Belgrade
stvar (fem.)	thing
taksi	taxi
to	that
umoran	tired
ustvari	in fact

večera	dinner
večeras	tonight
verovatno	probably
vrlo	very
zašto	why?
zašto da ne	why not?

GRAMMAR

This lesson features longer sentences and more complicated word order, and introduces a more colloquial register. The grammatical concepts will be discussed first to form the basis for a discussion of syntax and phraseology.

The noun *kola* "car" (pluralia tantum)

Kola (car) is a rare type of noun that does not have a singular form. Such a noun is called "pluralia tantum" and is similar to the English plural nouns "scissors" and "news." *Kola* is of neuter gender and its declension corresponds with the declension of neuter plural nouns.

Other pluralia tantum examples include:

makaze scissors (fem./pl.)
novine newspaper(s) (fem./pl.)
vrata door (neut./pl.)

The third case: Dative (singular and plural)

The third case, the dative, answers the question "to whom / to what (do I give)?" This case is used to indicate the indirect object of the verb. Its endings are almost always equivalent to the prepositional case endings. However, the prepositional indicates location (of an object) while the dative indicates movement towards something. If the dative is accompanied by a preposition, these are the prepositions *k, ka, prema* (toward).

The dative ending for singular masculine nouns is *-u*:

Govorim Robertu. I am telling Robert. (I am talking to Robert.)
Idemo prema hotelu. We are going toward the hotel.

The ending for singular feminine nouns is *-i*:

Govorim prijateljici. I am telling a female friend. (I am talking to a female friend.)

Idu prema Slaviji. They are going toward Slavija.

The singular neuter ending is *-u*:

Idemo prema moru. We are going toward the sea.

Certain neuter nouns, like the animate noun *dete*, take the consonant "t" before the ending *-u*:

Govorim detetu. I am telling the child. (I am talking to the child.)

N.B. These endings also apply to the prepositional singular (see Lesson Three).

Masculine and neuter plural nouns take the ending *-ima* in the dative (as for the instrumental and prepositional plural):

prijateljima; hotelima; selima; morima

Exception: As the neuter noun *dete* has no regular plural, its dative and prepositional plural form is *deci*.

Feminine nouns take the ending *-ma* in the dative plural:

prijateljicama; stjuardesama

The sixth case: Instrumental (exceptions)

In Lessons Two and Three we reviewed the instrumental singular and plural of nouns. We know that the instrumental answers the question "with whom / with what" and that most masculine nouns take the ending *-om* in the instrumental singular. Some masculine nouns that end with a vowel or a soft consonant take the ending *-em*:

Idem taksijem. I am going by taxi.
Idem sa prijateljem. I am going with a friend.

Taksi (taxi) is a masculine noun of foreign origin. It is an exception and is not declined in as many different cases as other masculine nouns. It also takes the consonant "j" before the case endings, e.g. *taksijem*. Its declension resembles the declension of masculine nouns ending in a soft consonant, such as *prijatelj* (friend).

Similarly, some neuter nouns take the ending *-em* instead of *-om* in the instrumental singular. These are usually neuter nouns ending in *-e* such as *more* (sea), whose instrumental form is *morem*. (The exception to this is the neuter noun *dete* that takes the consonant "t" before the instrumental ending *-om*: *detetom*.)

To review, masculine and neuter nouns take the ending *-ima* in the instrumental plural. Therefore:

Idemo kolima. We are going by car.

Remember that inanimate nouns, when indicating the means by which something is done, are not accompanied by prepositions (see Lesson Two). On the other hand, animate nouns such as *prijatelj* (indicating company/ friends), are accompanied by *s* or *sa* (with). This is a rule applying to the use of the instrumental case.

Declension of the personal pronouns *ja* "I" and *mi* "we"

Personal pronouns also change through the seven cases. All cases of the personal pronouns are given below. The personal pronoun *ja* (I) does not have the fifth case—the vocative (in singular or plural), which is used for calling or addressing someone (see Lesson Six).

	singular	*plural*
1. Nominative:	ja	mi
2. Genitive:	mene / me	nas
3. Dative:	meni / mi	nama / nam
4. Accusative:	mene / me	nas
5. Vocative:	—	—
6. Instrumental:	mnom	nama
7. Prepositional:	meni	nama

Some cases have a longer and a shorter version, as demonstrated above. The use of the short or long version depends on the position and emphasis of the pronoun in the sentence.

N.B. The short genitive and accusative singular forms *me* are pronounced "meh."

Declension of the personal pronouns *ti* and *vi* "you"

	singular	*plural*
1. Nominative:	ti	vi
2. Genitive:	tebe / te	vas
3. Dative:	tebi / ti	vama / vam
4. Accusative:	tebe / te	vas
5. Vocative:	ti!	vi!
6. Instrumental:	tobom	vama
7. Prepositional:	tebi	vama

The second-person plural *vi* is used when addressing more than one person, when addressing someone formally, or when one doesn't know the person very well.

The third-person pronouns ("he," "she," "it," and "they") are given in Lesson Seven.

Possessive adjectives

Certain adjectives are also used to express possession. Possessive adjectives can be made up of nouns—either personal names or animate nouns.

Jelenin brat. Jelena's brother.
Robertovo omiljeno mesto. Robert's favorite place.

To make up a possessive adjective with a feminine noun, the *-a* noun ending is replaced by the nominative singular adjective ending *-in*. The ending *-in* further acquires the endings *-a* and *-o* when the possessive adjective accompanies nouns of feminine and neuter gender respectively. See examples below.

Masculine nouns, for example the masculine name Robert, take the ending
-ov in the nominative singular, plus the ending *-o* when accompanying
neuter nouns, such as *mesto* (place).

Therefore possessive adjectives agree with the nouns that they modify in
gender, case, and number.

Nominative singular of possessive adjectives in each gender:

Jelenin prijatelj. Jelena's (male) friend.
Jelenina prijateljica. Jelena's (female) friend.
Jelenino omiljeno mesto. Jelena's favorite place.

Robertov prijatelj. Robert's (male) friend.
Robertova prijateljica. Robert's (female) friend.
Robertovo omiljeno mesto. Robert's favorite place.

Nominative plural in all three genders:

*Poss. adj. ending in -*in	*Poss. adj. ending in -*ov	
Jelenini prijatelji.	Robertovi prijatelji.	(masc.)
Jelenine prijateljice.	Robertove prijateljice.	(fem.)
Jelenina omiljena mesta.	Robertova omiljena mesta.	(neut.)

Masculine nouns ending in a vowel or a soft consonant (such as "ć," "dj,"
"j" or "š") take the ending *-ev* instead of *-ov*:

prijateljev prijatelj a friend's friend
prijateljeva prijateljica a friend's (female) friend
prijateljevo dete a friend's child

N.B. In this lesson's dialogue, the form *Kod Jeleninih roditelja* (At Jelena's
parents) is given. The noun *roditelji* (parents) is in the genitive plural, and
since the possessive adjective has to agree with the case of the noun, it takes
the genitive ending *-ih*. The declension of possessive adjectives and pronouns will be discussed in Lessons Six and Seven.

Ordinal number "one": *Prvi* "the first"

The ordinal number one acts as an adjective, agreeing with the noun:

nominative singular   *nominative plural*
prvi čas the first lesson   *prvi časovi* the first lessons   (masc.)
prva noć the first night   *prve noći* the first nights   (fem.)
prvo dete the first child   *prva deca* the first children   (neut.)

Prvi is declined like most other adjectives (see Lesson Seven).

Other ordinal numbers

The nominative singular masculine forms of the ordinal numbers one to four:

prvi, drugi, treći, četvrti

The nominative singular masculine forms of most other numbers are made by adding the ending *-i* to the cardinal number:

peti (the) fifth   *šesti* sixth
deseti tenth   *petnaesti* fifteenth
dvadeseti twentieth   *dvadeset peti* twenty-fifth

The cardinal numbers *sedam* and *osam* have the "fleeting a" and therefore their ordinal equivalents are:

sedmi (seventh) and *osmi* (eighth)

This also applies when they appear in compound numbers:

dvadeset sedmi, trideset osmi

The nominative singular feminine forms of the ordinal numbers take the ending -*a* instead of -*i*.

The nominative singular neuter forms take the ending -*o* instead of -*i*.

More ordinal numbers are listed in Lesson Eight under Explanations. Ordinal numbers are declined like most other adjectives (see Lesson Seven).

Adverbs

As in English, adverbs are words that modify verbs, adjectives, or other adverbs, and help to determine more specifically some of their characteristics. Adverbs in Serbo-Croat are often derived from adjectives, the neuter singular form of an adjective being used as the adverb:

puno a lot (from *pun, puna, puno*: full)
malo a little (from *mali, mala, malo*: small)
dobro well (from *dobar,-a,-o*: good)
dovoljno enough (from *dovoljan,-a,-o*: enough)
prvo first (from *prvi,-a,-o*: first)

Malo sam umoran. I am a little tired.

Here the adverb *malo* (a little) modifies the adjective *umoran* (tired). The sentence without the adverb would be:

Umoran sam. I am tired.

The adverb could have been added at the end of the sentence (with a change in word order): *Umoran sam malo*; however, the former expression is more natural.

First-class verbs

First-class verbs are the only verbs that can have either -*ći* or -*ti* as an infinitive ending. Verbs of all other classes have the infinitive ending -*ti*. This is because the verbs belonging to the first class are archaic verbs that have endured various phonetic changes over time.

The verbs *ići* and *moći*, for example, are first-class verbs ending in -*ći*. They formerly had the ending -*ti*, but with the development of the language the *t* has turned into *ć*. Verbs of the first class ending in -*ći* form a subgroup of their own—**1b**. Due to the apparent inconsistency of their infinitive stem endings, first-class verbs have more variations than any other class of verbs.

There are three subgroups within the first class of verbs. These are organized according to the morphology and phonetic changes of their stems and endings. The table below illustrates the differences between the subgroups:

	verb	*inf. stem*	*1ˢᵗ p. sing.*	*3ʳᵈ p. sing.*
1a	tresti (to shake)	tres-	tresem	tresu
1b	ići (to go)	id-	idem	idu
	peći (to bake)	pek-	pečem	peku
	moći (can)	mog-	mogu	mogu
1c	jesti (to eat)	jed-	jedem	jedu

The few verbs of the 1a subgroup can be identified by the infinitive stem ending -*s*. The verbs of the 1b subgroup have the recognizable infinitive ending -*ći*. The verbs of the 1c subgroup are recognizable by the infinitive stem ending -*d*. A variety of first-class verbs is presented below as well as in Lessons Six and Eight.

Present tense of the (class 1b) verb *moći* "can"

The imperfective verb *moći* (can) belongs to the first class of verbs, like the verb *ići* (to go). *Moći* takes the ending *-u* in the first-person singular of the present tense. The verbs *moći* and *hteti* (which also takes the *-u* ending) form exceptions in this respect.

Notice also that present tense stem of *moći* is irregular. This is also due to phonetic changes in the language. The present tense forms should be memorized:

singular	*plural*
ja mogu (I can)	mi možemo (we can)
ti možeš (you can)	vi možete (you can)
on može (he can)	oni mogu (they can)

The negative is formed by adding the particle *ne* in front of the relevant form of the verb:

ja ne mogu I can't
ona ne može she can't

Since *moći* can be used to express possibility or willingness, it corresponds to the modal verbs in the English language, such as "can," "may," "be able to."

Future tense of *moći* "can"

As we know, the future tense of the verb is formed by adding the short forms of the auxiliary verb *hteti* to the infinitive:

mi ćemo moći we will be able to
oni će moći they will be able to

In the short form, the infinitive of the verb *moći* remains, followed by the short forms of the verb *hteti*:

moći ću I'll be able to
moći ćemo we'll be able to

This is also the case with *ići* and other 1b class verbs whose infinitive ending is *-ći*, such as *reći* (to tell), *seći* (to cut):

ići ću I'll go
ići ćete you'll go
peći ću I'll bake

Remember that verbs which end in *-ti* in the infinitive normally lose that ending and take the short version of *hteti* as a suffix to make up the short form of the future tense (see Lesson Three). However, the 1b class verbs retain their full infinitive. In other words, the short form of 1b class verbs consists in dropping the pronoun from the long form and inverting the word order of the principal and auxiliary verbs.

The perfective (class 1c) verb *sesti* "to sit down"

Sesti (*sjesti* in ijek.) is also a first-class verb. It belongs to the 1c subgroup. Verbs of the 1c subgroup have the consonant *s* before the infinitive ending *-ti*, however (due to morphological and phonetic changes), their infinitive stem ends in *d*.

Other examples of 1c verbs are *jesti* (to eat) and *plesti* (to knit), etc. These verbs have particular endings in the present tense and they are best memorized separately. For example, the first-person singular of *jesti* in the present tense is *jedem*; whereas the first-person singular of *plesti* in the present tense is *pletem*. The conjugation of *jesti* (to eat) will be discussed in Lesson Eight.

The present tense conjugation of *sesti* (to sit down) is given below. Notice that it resembles the conjugation of third-class verbs rather than other first-class verbs:

sednem (I sit down)   sednemo (we sit down)
sedneš (you sit down)   sednete (you sit down)
sedne (he/she/it sits down)   sednu (they sit down)

The imperfective verb *sedati* "to sit down"

Sesti is a perfective verb. Its imperfective equivalent is *sedati*, which is a fifth-class verb:

sedam	sedamo
sedaš	sedate
seda	sedaju

Remember that imperfective verbs are used slightly differently from perfective verbs (see the previous lesson). However, please also note that *sesti* and *sedati* are not durative verbs. (*Sedam* could be translated as "I'm taking a seat," whereas *Želim da sednem* could mean "I'd like to sit down.") They both indicate only the completed action of taking a seat. The imperfective fifth-class verb *sedeti* is a durative verb that means "to be sitting" and therefore indicates the state of sitting down.

Odsesti and *odsedati* "to stay"

When the prefix *od-* is added to the infinitives *sesti* or *sedati*, the verb changes meaning. The perfective *odsesti* and the imperfective *odsedati*—both meaning "to stay"—indicate specific accommodation (as mentioned in Lesson Three) and are used only in this context:

*Gde vi odsedate?** Where are you staying?
Ja ću odsesti u hotelu. I'll stay in a hotel.

*As we have seen, the use of imperfective verbs in the present tense can indicate future meaning. This is not the case with perfective verbs. The future tense of perfective verbs can only be built using the infinitive and the auxiliary verb *hteti* (as in the example above).

Future tense of *sesti* "to sit"

The long form of the future tense is built as normal:

Ja ću sesti. I will sit down.
Mi ćemo sesti. We will sit down.
Etc.

The short future tense form of *sesti* requires the infinitive stem of the verb (derived by dropping the infinitive ending *-ti*). The short forms of the auxiliary verb *hteti* are then added to the infinitive stem *ses-*. Because of particular phonetic rules in Serbo-Croat, the consonant *ć* next to the consonant *s* turns the *s* into the consonant *š*.

sešću	sešćemo
sešćeš	sešćete
sešće	sešće

Second-class verbs

Second-class verbs have an infinitive stem that ends in *-a* (*pisa-ti* "to write," *kaza-ti* "to tell," etc.). In the present tense they lose this ending *-a* and acquire the present tense endings *-em, -eš, -e, -emo, -ete, -u*.

Due to particular phonetic rules, the resultant infinitive stem endings *-s* and *-z* in the examples above change into *š* and *ž* respectively:

pišem I write
kažem I tell

This phonetic alteration does not apply to all other second-class verbs (see below).

The second-class verb *zvati* "to call"

Zvati (to call) is an imperfective second-class verb. Its infinitive stem is *zva-*, with the ending *-a* that disappears in the present tense. The stem then acquires the vowel *o* before its last consonant: *zov-*. The present tense endings (*-em, -eš, -e, -emo, -ete, -u*) are added onto this stem:

zovem (I call)	zovemo (we call)
zoveš (you call)	zovete (you call)
zove (he/she/it calls)	zovu (they call)

The reflexive particle *se* accompanies the verb in the following phrases:

Kako se zovete? What is your name? (lit.: What do you call yourself?)
Zovem se . . . My name is . . . (lit.: I call myself . . .)

Pozvati and *pozivati* "to invite"

When accompanied by the prefix *po-*, the verb *zvati* forms the result *pozvati* (to invite).

Pozvati, however, is perfective and cannot be used in the present tense on its own. Therefore it must appear with another verb:

Želim da vas pozovem na piće. I wish / would like to invite you for a drink.

Its imperfective equivalent, the fifth-class verb *pozivati* (to invite), would be used in its place in an independent sentence:

Pozivam vas na piće večeras. I invite you for a drink tonight.

N.B. Both *pozvati* and *pozivati* are transitive verbs (see discussion below).

Reflexive verbs

Reflexive verbs are those which have the subject as an object. They are accompanied by two pronouns of the same person: a subject pronoun (which can be implied by the inflection of the verb) and an object pronoun.

Ja se češljam. or *Češljam se.* I am combing myself.

The subject pronoun is *ja* and the object pronoun (which also denotes the subject) is *se*.

The object pronoun *se* is called the reflexive particle and does not change form. In dictionaries, the infinitive of reflexive verbs is always accompanied by this particle *se*.

Dogovoriti se (to make an agreement / arrangement) is a perfective sixth-class reflexive verb.

Dogovorićemo se. We'll make an arrangement.

Because *dogovoriti se* is a perfective verb and therefore indicates an action that is complete or limited in time, the meaning of the above example does not indicate a process of making an arrangement but the fact that the arrangement will be made.

For the same reasons of duration, in the present tense, perfective verbs are always accompanied by the copula *da*. Therefore *dogovoriti se* often accompanies a modal verb and either appears in its infinitive form or in the relevant (inflected) present tense form preceded by the copula *da*:

Možemo se dogovoriti. We can make an arrangement.
Možemo da se dogovorimo. We can make an arrangement.

Notice that the reflexive particle *se* precedes the verb.

Similarly, *pridružiti se* (to join) is a perfective sixth-class reflexive verb. This verb, however, also requires another object:

Pridružiću vam se. I will join you.

Here the object is placed between the verb and the reflexive particle. This is because the object is actually a personal pronoun (the dative plural of the personal pronoun *vi* "you"). If the object was named, then the sentence could only be phrased thus:

Pridružiću se Robertu. I will join Robert.

The object (*Robert*) of the verb *pridružiti se* (to join) is always in the dative case.

Being a perfective verb, *pridružiti se* in the present tense can only appear as a secondary verb in the infinitive or when preceded by the copula *da*:

Mogu vam se pridružiti. I can join you. (or: I may join you.)
Mogu li da vam se pridružim? Can I join you? (May I join you?)
*Možda vam se pridružim.** Maybe I'll join you.

*The adverb *možda* (maybe, perhaps), derived from the verb *moći* and the copula *da*, can precede the present tense of a perfective verb in the place of a modal verb and the copula *da*.

If the object in this sentence (*vam*) was replaced by a name or a noun, the sentence would look like this:

Mogu se pridružiti Robertu. / Mogu da se pridružim Robertu.
     I can join Robert.

Word order with reflexive verbs

Notice that in the examples above featuring a noun as the object of the verb, the word order with the reflexive verb is thus:

* subject / inflected modal verb + reflexive particle + infinitive of the perfective verb (reflexive) + object (noun)

     Mogu + se + pridružiti + Robertu.

Or:

* subject / inflected modal verb + copula *da* + reflexive particle + inflected perfective verb (reflexive) + object (noun)

     Mogu + da + se + pridružim + Robertu.

In the examples featuring the personal pronoun as an object, the word order is as follows:

- subject / inflected modal verb + object (pronoun) + reflexive particle + infinitive of perfective verb

  Mogu + vam + se + pridružiti.

Or:

- subject / inflected modal verb + copula *da* + object (pronoun) + reflexive particle + inflected perfective verb

  Mogu + da + vam + se + pridružim.

The inflected modal verb indicates the subject through its inflection. However, if it is important for the subject to be stated, there would be several possibilities:

I can join you.
Ja vam se mogu pridružiti.
Mogu vam se ja pridružiti.
Ja mogu da vam se pridružim.
Mogu ja da vam se pridružim.

All of these examples emphasize the subject, indicating that it is selected from a variety of possible subjects. The above examples do not represent any rules; rather, they demonstrate that word order can be much more flexible in Serbo-Croat, depending on what needs to be emphasized.

It would be equally possible to emphasize the object, by using the longer dative form *vama* of the pronoun *vi*, thus:

I can join you.
Mogu se vama pridružiti.
Mogu se pridružiti vama.
Mogu da se vama pridružim.
Mogu da se pridružim vama.

Or, as in the example featured in the dialogue:

Možete se vi nama pridružiti. You can join us.

Here the emphasis is both on the subject and the object: "<u>You</u> can join <u>us</u>" as opposed to "us joining you."

Transitive verbs

Transitive verbs are verbs that require an object. The object is most often in the accusative case (but can be in the genitive or the dative). Such verbs are: *imati* (to have), *nemati* (not to have), *piti* (to drink), etc.

Pijem kafu. I am drinking coffee.

Another transitive verb is *baciti* (to throw) or its derivative *odbaciti* (to throw off), also meaning "to give someone a lift."

Možemo vas odbaciti do hotela. We can give you a lift to the hotel.

N.B. *Odbaciti* (like *baciti*) is a perfective sixth-class verb that is conjugated like the verb *raditi* (to do, to work).

Word order with transitive verbs

In the example above the transitive verb *odbaciti* is accompanied by the accusative form of the personal pronoun *vi* "you" (*vas*). The object precedes the verb because the emphasis in this sentence is not on the object.

It is possible to construct the sentence with the object pronoun after the verb:

Možemo odbaciti <u>vas</u> do hotela.

In this sentence, the emphasis moves to the object, indicating that the object is selected out of a number of possible objects.

If the object was a personal name or a noun, the object would more naturally follow the verb in the sentence:

Možemo odbaciti <u>Marka</u> do hotela.

Word order:

- subject / inflected modal verb + object (pronoun) in the accusative + verb (transitive) in the infinitive + adverbial determiner (optional)

Or:

- subject / inflected modal verb + verb (transitive) in the infinitive + object (noun) in the accusative + adverbial determiner (optional)

The example given is a compound sentence in which the subject is "we," the main verb is the modal verb "can," and the secondary sentence is "give you a lift to the hotel." Of course, it would be possible to say:

Odbacićemo vas do hotela. We will give you a lift to the hotel.

But the function of this sentence is different as it gives little or no choice to the object and no longer constitutes a formal offer.

The general rule is: when a secondary verb in a compound sentence is accompanied by a personal pronoun as the object, the word order is changed so that the personal pronoun precedes the secondary verb.

A more complicated example of this from the dialogue above:

Onda ćete mi dozvoliti da vas pozovem na piće večeras. Then you will allow me to invite you for a drink tonight.

Here the verb *dozvoliti* (to allow) is preceded by the object—the dative form *mi* of the personal pronoun *ja* (I). The transitive verb *pozvati* (to invite) is preceded by the accusative form *vas* of the personal pronoun *vi* (you), as the object in the secondary sentence.

It would be possible to phrase the same sentence thus:

Dozvolićete mi da vas pozovem na piće večeras. You will allow me to invite you for a drink tonight.

Here the personal pronoun in the dative case follows the main verb *dozvoliti* (to allow) and is followed by the secondary sentence *da vas pozovem na piće* (to invite you for a drink).

The adverb *onda* (then) at the beginning of the given example causes a reversal of the word order. The main sentence *dozvolićete mi* (you will allow me) becomes a secondary sentence in relation to the previous part of the conversation to which the adverb relates. In other words, the following sentence indicates a conditional structure:

Onda ćete mi dozvoliti da vas pozovem na piće.

In the dialogue above it is a response to the offer of a lift. The entire thought expressed by the sentence is:

If you insist on giving me a lift, then you will allow me to invite you for a drink.

The future tense used as the imperative

The imperative in Serbo-Croat, as in English, can be expressed through the use of the future tense:

Dozvolićete mi da vas pozovem na piće. You will allow me to invite you for a drink.

Prvo ćete se odmorititi. First you will take a rest.

This is a mild imperative, used in polite register to give instructions or to make a strong, insistent request.

The building of the proper grammatical imperative will be discussed in Lesson Six.

ADDITIONAL EXPLANATIONS

Nouns followed by a name

Odsešću u hotelu "Slavija." I'll stay in the hotel "Slavija."

After the word "hotel" used in the prepositional case, the name of the hotel is in the nominative or, when used alone, in the prepositional case.

Odsešću u "Slaviji." I'll stay at the "Slavija."

This generally applies to names of hotels, restaurants, as well as book titles, etc.

Imam knjigu "Romeo i Julija." I have the book *Romeo and Juliet.*

Imam "Romea i Juliju." I have *Romeo and Juliet.*

Impersonal use of *imati* "to have"

Ima dovoljno prostora. There is enough space.

The use of *imati* (to have) in the third-person singular, without an apparent subject, can indicate the existence or presence of something, as demonstrated above. The verb is then accompanied by the noun (*prostor* "space") in the genitive (*prostora*).

Ima li ovde dobrih hotela? Are there any good hotels around here?

USEFUL PHRASES

Želim da odsednem u hotelu. Ima li ovde dobrih hotela?
(ZHELlim-dah ODsednem u-hotEHloo. IMmah-lih OHOvdeh DOBbrihh
   hotELlah)
I want to stay at a hotel. Are there any good hotels around here?

Oni idu taksijem, ja idem kolima.
(oni-IDdoo TAHksiyem, yah-IDdem KOHLlimah)
They are going by taxi, I am going by car.

Je li taksi skup na aerodromu?
(yeh-lih TAHksi skoop nah-AHEHrodromu)
Is a taxi expensive at the airport?

- Možete nam se pridružiti na večeri.
- Zašto da ne?
   (MOHzhetteh nam-seh priDROOzhittih na-hVEHcherih)
   (ZAHshtoh-dah NEH)
- You can join us for dinner tonight.
- Why not?

Dogovorićemo se.
(doggovVOHrichemoh-seh)
We'll arrange something.

EXERCISES

I. Answer the questions.

1. Gde odseda Marko?
2. Gde odsedaju Robert i Jelena?
3. Ko čeka Roberta i Jelenu na aerodromu?
4. Gde idu Robert i Jelena večeras?˙
5. Hoće li se Marko pridružiti Robertu i Jeleni?

II. Turn the following statements into questions using all the possible ways you know.

1. Taksi na aerodromu je vrlo skup.
2. Dozvolićete mi da vas pozovem na piće.
3. Možete nam se pridružiti na večeri.
4. Skadarlija je Robertovo omiljeno mesto u Beogradu.
5. Ima dovoljno prostora u kolima.

III. Decline the following nouns in all the cases you know.

stvar (fem.)
večera (fem.)
mesto (neut.)
makaze (fem. pl.) – scissors
vrata (neut. pl.) – door

IV. Conjugate the following two verbs in the present and future tense.

pozvati (2nd Cl.) – to invite
odmoriti se (6th Cl.) – to take a rest

V. Make up five sentences using words and phrases you have learned.

LESSON SIX

DIALOGUE

Na Aerodromu

STJUARDESA:	Poštovani putnici, molimo vas vežite se, slećemo. Nadamo se da ste imali ugodan let.
JELENA:	Marko, koliko dugo niste bili u Jugoslaviji?
MARKO:	Dve godine. Molim vas predjite na "ti," ne morate da mi persirate.
ROBERT:	Onda i vi morate da predjete na "ti."
MARKO:	Važi. Jesmo li sleteli?
JELENA:	Mislim da jesmo. Roberte, gde su nam pasoši?
ROBERT:	U tvojoj tašni.
JELENA:	Ah, da, u pravu si. Idemo!
STJUARDESA:	Dovidjenja. Prijatno.
SVI:	Hvala. Dovidjenja.

PASOŠKA KONTROLA:	Vaše pasoše molim?
JELENA:	Izvolite.
P. KONTROLA:	Gospodin je stranac?
JELENA:	Da. Gospodin je moj suprug.
P. KONTROLA:	Ima li vizu?
ROBERT:	Da, sve je u redu.
P. KONTROLA:	Nema problema. Hvala. Dovidjenja.

At the Airport

STEWARDESS:	Dear passengers, please put your seat belts on, we are landing. We hope you've had a pleasant journey.
JELENA:	Marko, how long have you not been in Yugoslavia?
MARKO:	Two years. Please, go onto saying "ti," you don't have to be formal with me.
ROBERT:	Then you also have to go onto saying "ti."
MARKO:	OK. Have we landed?
JELENA:	I think we have. Robert, where are our passports?
ROBERT:	In your handbag.
JELENA:	Ah, yes, you are right. Let's go!
STEWARDESS:	Good-bye. Have a nice time.
ALL:	Thank you. Good-bye.
PASSPORT CONTROL:	Your passports, please?
JELENA:	Here you are.
P. CONTROL:	The gentleman is a foreigner?
JELENA:	Yes. The gentleman is my husband.
P. CONTROL:	Does he have a visa?
ROBERT:	Yes, everything is all right.
P. CONTROL:	All right. Thank you. Good-bye.

MARKO:	Jeste li našli svoj prtljag?
JELENA:	Ja još uvek čekam. Robert je otišao po kolica. Tebe su zadržali na pasoškoj kontroli?
MARKO:	Da, zato što imam dvojno državljanstvo. Hteli su da vide oba pasoša.
JELENA:	A, ovo su naše torbe. Molim te, Marko, možeš li mi pomoći?
MARKO:	Svakako. Je li ovaj crni kofer vaš? A evo i moje torbe!
ROBERT:	Tačno na vreme!
CARINIK:	Imate li nešto da prijavite za carinu?
JELENA:	Moj suprug ima samo lični laptop.
MARKO:	A ja imam samo lični foto-aparat.
CARINIK:	U redu. Prodjite. Dovidjenja.
JELENA:	A, eno Vlade! Vlado!
VLADA:	Zdravo! Kako ste putovali?
ROBERT:	Odlično. Da te upoznamo: ovo je Marko, naš saputnik, ovo je Vlada, Jelenin brat.
JELENA:	Ubedili smo Marka da krene sa nama kolima. On ide na Slaviju.
VLADA:	Drago mi je. Idemo, onda.

MARKO:	Have you found your luggage yet?
JELENA:	I am still waiting. Robert went to find a baggage cart. They kept you at the passport control?
MARKO:	Yes, because I have dual citizenship. They wanted to see both passports.
JELENA:	Ah, these are our bags. Please, Marko, can you help me?
MARKO:	By all means. Is this black suitcase yours? And there's my bag too!
ROBERT:	Just in time!

CUSTOMS OFFICER:	Have you got anything to declare?
JELENA:	My husband only has a personal laptop.
MARKO:	And I only have a personal camera.
CUSTOMS OFFICER:	All right. You can go through. Good-bye.

JELENA:	Ah, there's Vlada! Vlada!
Vlada:	Hello! Did you have a good journey?
ROBERT:	Excellent! Let me introduce you: this is Marko, our co-passenger, this is Vlada, Jelena's brother.
JELENA:	We've persuaded Marko to come with us in the car. He is going to Slavija.
MARKO:	I'm glad. Let's go then.

VOCABULARY

carina (fem.)	customs
carinik (masc.)	customs officer
crn,-a,-o	black
čekati (Cl. 5)	to wait
dvojno državljanstvo	dual citizenship
eno	there is
evo	here is
foto-aparat (masc.)	camera
godina (fem.)	year
gospodin	gentleman
još uvek	still
kofer (masc.)	suitcase
kolica	baggage cart, trolley
krenuti (Cl. 3)	to come, to set off
ličan,-a,-o	personal
misliti (Cl. 6)	to think
morati (Cl. 5)	to have to, must
naći (Cl. 1)	to find
naš,-a,-e	our
nadati se (Cl. 5)	to hope
nema problema	no problem
oba	both
otići (Cl. 1)	to go, to depart
ovaj,-a,-o	this
ovo	this
pasoš (masc.)	passport
pasoška kontrola	passport control
persirati (Cl. 5)	to address someone formally, with *vi*
po	for
pomoći (Cl. 1)	to help
preći (Cl. 1)	to go onto, to cross (over)
prijaviti (Cl. 6)	to declare
proći (Cl. 1)	to go through
prtljag (masc.)	luggage

putovati (Cl. 4)	to travel
samo	only
saputnik (masc.)	co-passenger
sleteti (Cl. 6)	to land (by plane)
stranac (masc.)	foreigner
svakako	by all means
sve	everything
svoj,-a,-e	one's, yours
(reflexive possessive pronoun)	
tačno na vreme	exactly on time
tašna (fem.)	handbag
ti	of
torba (fem.)	bag
tvoj,-a,-e	your
u pravu si	you are right
u redu	all right (lit.: in order)
ubediti (Cl. 6)	to persuade
upoznati (Cl. 5)	to introduce, to get to know, to meet
važi	OK, all right, agreed
vezati se (Cl. 2)	to tie oneself, (to put the seat belt on)
videti (Cl. 6)	to see
viza (fem.)	visa
zadržati (Cl. 6)	to keep
zato što	because

EXPLANATIONS

Ways of addressing

• We have already discussed the polite / formal forms of address that use the second-person plural *vi*. In Serbo-Croat this is called *persiranje*. The verb indicating this action of formal address is *persirati*. If one wishes to invite someone to start addressing them in a more informal or friendly way, the following phrases can be used:

Ne morate da mi persirate.	(formal)
You don't have to address me formally.	
Ne moraš da mi persiraš.	(informal)
You don't have to address me formally.	
Nemojte mi persirati.	(formal)
Please, don't address me formally.	
Nemoj mi persirati.	(informal)
Don't address me formally.	

As you can see from the examples above, it is possible to invite someone to address one informally in a formal or an informal way. This is because the subject may decide that he/she does not wish to be addressed formally but still wishes to address the other person formally. Often younger people may invite an older person to address them informally while continuing to address that person formally. The invitation often needs to come from both sides. If both parties are young people of a similar age, they may decide to put the invitation forward so that it applies to both sides:

Nećemo persirati jedno drugom. We won't be addressing one another formally.
Da ne persiramo jedno drugom. Let's not address one another formally.
Da predjemo na "ti." Let's go on to (saying) "ti."

(The verb *nemoj* "don't" is discussed at the end of this lesson.)

- Men are addressed with the noun *gospodin* in the vocative form *gospodine* (the accent is on the second syllable—gossPODineh). The noun *gospodin* can be used either on its own (like "sir" in English) or followed by the first or second name of the person:

Gospodine Roberte . . . or *Gospodine Petroviću . . .*

Notice that the name is always in the vocative case.

- Married women are addressed with the noun *gospodja* in the vocative form *gospodjo* (pronounced as "GOSSpodyoh"). *Gospodja* can be used on its own (like "madam" in English) or followed by the first or second name of the person:

Gospodjo Jelena . . . or *Gospodjo Petrović . . .*

Notice that when addressing a woman the surname stays in the nominative case.

- Young women are addressed with the noun *gospodjica* in the vocative form *gospodjice* (pronounced as "GOSSpodyitseh"). The noun *gospodjica* can be used on its own or followed by the first or second name:

Gospodjice Jelena . . . or *Gospodjice Petrović . . .*

When a group of people is addressed, a number of terms can be used:

Dame i gospodo
(DAAHmeh-ih-GOSSpodoh)
Ladies and gentlemen

Poštovani . . .
(POSHtovanni)
Respected . . . / Dear . . .

Dragi . . .
(drAAHgee)
Dear . . .

The latter two are normally used when addressing a group of people, such as guests (*dragi gosti*), passengers (*poštovani putnici*), etc. The adjectives *poštovani* and *dragi* are followed here by a masculine plural noun.

In the communist era, different forms of address were used. Terms such as *gospodine*, *gospodjo*, *dame i gospodo* were dismissed as being bourgeois. Their use has reemerged in the last ten years. The communist register favored the terms *druže*, *drugarice*, and *drugovi i drugarice*, which corresponded with the term "comrade" (in masculine singular, feminine singular, and plural respectively). The nouns *drug* and *drugarica* also mean "a (school) friend" (masculine and feminine respectively).

GRAMMAR

The fifth case: Vocative

The vocative case of the noun is used for calling or addressing. It is most often used with personal names or official titles, however, inanimate nouns take the vocative form too. Masculine nouns ending in a consonant most commonly have the vocative ending -*e*:

profesore! Roberte! Beograde!

Masculine nouns ending in a soft consonant such as *ć, dj, j* or *š* take the ending -*u*:

prijatelju! Petroviću!

Masculine nouns ending in a vowel usually stay the same as in the nominative case:

Nikola! Marko!

Some short masculine names ending in -*a* take the ending -*o* in the vocative:

Vlado! Čedo!

Feminine nouns ending in a vowel most commonly take the ending -*o*:

gospodjo! stjuardeso!

Feminine nouns and names ending in -*ica* have the ending -*e* in the vocative singular:

prijateljice! Milice!

Feminine personal names normally stay the same as in the nominative:

Jelena! Marija!

Some short feminine names ending in *-a* take the ending *-o* in the vocative:

Majo! Neno!

Feminine nouns ending in a consonant take the ending *-i*:

noći!

The vocative form of neuter nouns is equivalent to their nominative form.

The vocative plural form of all nouns is equivalent to their nominative plural form.

Declension of the interrogative pronouns *ko* "who" and *šta* "what"

1. Nominative: ko   šta
2. Genitive: koga   čega
3. Dative: kome   čemu
4. Accusative: koga   šta
5. Vocative: —   —
6. Instrumental: kim   čim
7. Prepositional: kome   čemu

The interrogative pronouns *ko* (who) and *šta* (what) do not have a plural nor a vocative form.

Declension of the possessive pronoun *moj* "my"

	singular			plural		
	masc.	*neut.*	*fem.*	*masc.*	*neut.*	*fem.*
Nom.:	moj	moje	moja	moji	moja	moje
Gen.:	mojeg(a)/mog(a)	"	moje	mojih	"	mojih
Dat.:	mojem(u)/mom(e)	"	mojoj	mojim(a)	"	mojim
Acc.:	moj/mog(a)*	moje	moju	moje	moja	moje
Voc.:	moj	moje	moja	moji	moja	moje
Instr.:	mojim	"	mojom	mojim(a)	"	mojim
Prep.:	mojem(u)/mom(e)	"	mojoj	mojim(a)	"	mojim

Note that some cases have longer and shorter forms. In everyday conversation the shorter forms are used more frequently (the longer forms have archaic connotations). However, the use of the particular form also depends on the noun that it accompanies.

*The accusative singular masculine form is equivalent to the nominative singular masculine form if the pronoun accompanies an inanimate object, and to the genitive singular if it accompanies a living being:

Vidim moj grad. I see my town.
Vidim mog prijatelja. I see my friend.

In the example above, both nouns are in the accusative case but they have different accusative forms (and also take different forms of the possessive pronoun).

Note that this only applies to the accusative of <u>masculine</u> nouns in the <u>singular</u>.

Declension of the possessive pronoun *tvoj* "your"

	masc.	*neut.*	*fem.*	*masc.*	*neut.*	*fem.*
		singular			plural	
Nom.:	tvoj	tvoje	tvoja	tvoji	tvoja	tvoje
Gen.:	tvojeg(a)/tvog(a)	"	tvoje	tvojih	"	tvojih
Dat.:	tvojem(u)/tvom(e)	"	tvojoj	tvojim(a)	"	tvojim
Acc.:	tvoj/tvog(a)	tvoje	tvoju	tvoje	tvoja	tvoje
Voc.:	tvoj	tvoje	tvoja	tvoji	tvoja	tvoje
Instr.:	tvojim	"	tvojom	tvojim(a)	"	tvojim
Prep.:	tvojem(u)/tvom(e)	"	tvojoj	tvojim(a)	"	tvojim

Declension of the possessive pronoun *naš* "our"

	masc.	*neut.*	*fem.*	*masc.*	*neut.*	*fem.*
		singular			plural	
Nom.:	naš	naše	naša	naši	naša	naše
Gen.:	našeg(a)	"	naše	naših	"	naših
Dat.:	našem(u)	"	našoj	našim(a)	"	našim
Acc.:	= Nom. / Gen.	=Nom.	našu	naše	=Nom.	=Nom.
Voc.:	=Nom.	=Nom.	=Nom.	=Nom.	=Nom.	=Nom.
Instr.:	našim	"	našom	=Dat.	=Dat.	=Dat.
Prep.:	=Dat.	=Dat.	=Dat.	=Dat.	=Dat.	=Dat.

Declension of the possessive pronoun *vaš* "your"

	masc.	*neut.*	*fem.*	*masc.*	*neut.*	*fem.*
		singular			plural	
Nom.:	vaš	vaše	vaša	vaši	vaša	vaše
Gen.:	vašeg(a)	"	vaše	vaših	"	vaših
Dat.:	vašem(u)	"	vašoj	vašim(a)	"	vašim
Acc.:	=Nom. / Gen.	=Nom.	vašu	vaše	=Nom.	=Nom.
Voc.:	=Nom.	=Nom.	=Nom.	=Nom.	=Nom.	=Nom.
Instr.:	vašim	"	vašom	=Dat.	=Dat.	=Dat.
Prep.:	=Dat.	=Dat.	=Dat.	=Dat.	=Dat.	=Dat.

N.B. Some forms are used in Croatian more than in Serbian, such as the dative and the prepositional singular ending with *-u*: *mojemu*, *tvojemu*, *našemu*, and *vašemu*.

The possessive reflexive pronoun *svoj* "one's own"

The possessive pronoun *svoj* is used when the subject of the sentence is referred to as the possessor. It is used with any person and replaces other possessive pronouns (*moj*, *tvoj*, etc.) It is declined like the possessive pronoun *moj*.

Čekam svoj prtljag. I am waiting for my (own) luggage.
Jeste li našli svoj prtljag? Have you found your luggage?

Definite and indefinite adjectives

We already know that adjectives in Serbo-Croat are inflected to agree in gender, number, and case with the noun they accompany. Most adjectives also have a definite and indefinite form. However, some adjectives such as possessive ones ending in *-ov* and *-in* (*Markov*, *Jelenin*) only have an indefinite form.

The indefinite form of the adjective can function as a predicate, accompanying the verb *jesam*:

Robert je lep. Robert is handsome.
Kofer je crn. The suitcase is black.
Prtljag je Jelenin. The luggage is Jelena's.

The definite form of the adjective is often used to describe the subjective noun more closely:

Ovaj lepi čovek je Robert. This handsome man is Robert.
Je li ovaj crni kofer vaš? Is this black suitcase yours?

Notice that the indefinite masculine adjectives end in a consonant, whereas the definite masculine adjectives end in *-i*.

Both definite and indefinite adjectives of the feminine gender end in -*a*:

lepa, crna

Both definite and indefinite adjectives of the neuter gender end in -*o*:

lepo, crno

Some adjectives only take the definite form. Such adjectives include *mali* (small) and *veliki* (big).

Also adjectives ending in -*ni*, which are often derived from nouns, only take the definite form. These adjectives include *voćni* (fruity), *lični* (personal), *narodni* (national), etc.

Because they do not have an indefinite form, these adjectives can be used as predicates:

Moj kofer je mali. My suitcase is small.
Beograd nije veliki. Belgrade isn't big.
Ovaj sok je voćni. This juice is fruit (juice).
Imam samo lični laptop. I only have a personal laptop.

Please note that in polite/formal conversation, if the adjective is used predicatively, it always assumes the masculine plural regardless of the gender of the addressed person:

Vi ste lepi. You are handsome (beautiful).

N.B. In questions featuring the interrogative pronoun *ko* (who)—where the subject is unknown—the indefinite adjective in the masculine gender is used:

Ko je lep? Who is beautiful?

And exceptionally:

Ko je mali? Who is small?

On the other hand, in questions featuring the pronoun *šta* (what), the indefinite adjective is in the neuter gender:

Šta je lepo? What is beautiful?
Šta je malo? What is small?

Demonstrative adverbs *evo, eto* "here" and *eno* "there"

Evo and *eto* (here) and *eno* (there) are used to indicate that something or someone is near or approaching. These adverbs are always followed by a noun in the genitive case:

Evo moje torbe. Here's my bag.
Eno Vlade. There's Vlada.

More first-class verbs

Otići (to go away), *proći* (to go through), and *preći* (to go over) are all perfective verbs derived from the verb *ići*. Their conjugations are slightly different from that of *ići*. *Otići* has several present tense conjugations (both archaic and modern). Two are presented here:

archaic		*modern*	
otidjem	otidjemo	odem	odemo
otidješ	otidjete	odeš	odete
otidje	otidju	ode	odu

The verbs *preći* and *proći* have similar conjugations:

predjem	predjemo	prodjem	prodjemo
predješ	predjete	prodješ	prodjete
predje	predju	prodje	prodju

So does the perfective verb *naći* (to find):

nadjem, nadješ, etc.

The perfective verb *pomoći* (to help) has a slightly different present tense conjugation:

pomognem   pomognemo
pomogneš   pomognete
pomogne   pomognu

The future tense of these verbs is formed simply like the future of the verb *moći* (can), demonstrated in the previous lesson.

N.B. The imperfective equivalents of the above verbs are: *odlaziti* (Cl. 6), *prelaziti* (Cl. 6), *prolaziti* (Cl. 6), *nalaziti* (Cl. 6) and *pomagati* (Cl. 3—although its conjugation resembles Cl. 2 verbs: *pomažem, pomažeš*, etc.).

Second-class (b) verbs

Second-class verbs divide into two subgroups. The verb *zvati* (to call), which we reviewed earlier (see Lesson Five), falls into the first subgroup (2a).

The second subgroup (2b) consists of verbs whose infinitive stem finishes with *a* preceded by the consonants *s* or *z*, such as *pisa-ti* (to write), *kaza-ti* (to tell), *veza-ti* (to tie). However, because of a particular phonetic rule, the *s* and *z* in the stem, in combination with the personal endings, turn into *š* and *ž* respectively. (Alternatively the present stem can end with a *t* that turns into *ć* or an *l* that turns into *lj*.)

pisati (to write)   *vezati* (to tie)

pišem   pišemo   vežem   vežemo
pišeš   pišete _   vežeš   vežete
piše   pišu   veže   vežu

The future tense forms of these verbs are unaffected by the above phonetic rules:

pisaću, pisaćemo, vezaću, vezaćemo, etc.

N.B. *Pisati* is an imperfective verb, *vezati* is a perfective verb whose imperfective equivalent is *vezivati* (Cl. 4b—*vezujem* . . .).

Third-class verbs

The verbs of the third class have an infinitive stem ending in *-nu*, such as *krenu-ti* (to set off, to go) and *brinu-ti* (to worry). In the present tense, they lose the ending *-u* from the infinitive stem in all but the third-person plural and conjugate as follows:

krenuti (to set off, to go)

krenem (I go)	krenemo (we go)
kreneš (you go)	krenete (you go)
krene (he/she/it goes)	krenu (they go)

The infinitive stem of third-class verbs retains the ending *-nu* in other tenses. For example, the future tense is formed using the infinitive stem and relevant endings:

krenuću, krenućemo, etc.

N.B. *Krenuti* is a perfective verb and its imperfective form is *kretati* (Cl. 2b)—*krećem, krećeš, kreće, krećemo, krećete, kreću.*

Fourth-class (b) verbs

Fourth-class verbs divide into two subgroups. The verb *piti* (to drink) belongs to the 4a class of verbs (see Lesson Two). Class four verbs also include verbs such as *stanovati* (to dwell, to live) and *putovati* (to travel). These verbs belong to the 4b class of verbs. The infinitive stem of the 4b class of verbs ends in *-ova*. In the present tense, the ending *-ova* is dropped from the infinitive stem and replaced by the ending *-u*. Therefore:

putovati (to travel)

putujem (I travel)	putujemo (we travel)
putuješ (you travel)	putujete (you travel)
putuje (he/she/it travels)	putuju (they travel)

However, the infinitive stem ending in -*ova* remains intact in other tenses. Therefore, the future tense is built as usual, by dropping the ending -*ti* from the infinitive and adding the relevant suffixes:

putovaću, putovaćemo, etc.

Fifth-class verbs

As discussed in Lesson Two, fifth-class verbs have an infinitive stem that ends in short "a" and a present stem that ends in long "a," such as *imati* (to have) (*imam* . . .), *znati* (to know), *morati* (must, to have to), and *nadati se* (to hope). Since *nadati se* is a reflexive verb, it does not appear without the particle *se*:

nadati se (to hope)   *morati* (must, to have to)

nadam se	nadamo se	moram	moramo
nadaš se	nadate se	moraš	morate
nada se	nadaju se	mora	moraju

N.B. *Ne morati,* the negative form of *morati,* has the meaning of "need not" or "not have to" and NOT the meaning of "must not."

Sixth-class verbs

Verbs of the sixth class divide into three subgroups. The first subgroup contains verbs whose infinitive stem ends in -*i* and whose present stem also ends in -*i*: *raditi* (to do, to work) (*radim* . . .), *ubediti* (to persuade).

The second subgroup includes verbs whose infinitive stem ends in -*e* and whose present stem ends in -*i*: *živeti* (to live) (*živim* . . .), *videti* (to see), *leteti* (to fly):

videti (to see)   *leteti* (to fly)

vidim	vidimo	letim	letimo
vidiš	vidite	letiš	letite
vidi	vide	leti	lete

The third subgroup—sometimes referred to as the seventh class of verbs—includes verbs whose infinitive stem ends in -a and whose present stem ends in long -i: *držati* (to hold) (*držim* . . .), *zadržati* (to keep sbd/sth):

zadržati (to keep sbd/sth)

zadržim	zadržimo
zadržiš	zadržite
zadrži	zadrže

The future tense of sixth-class verbs is built as usual, using the infinitive stem and relevant endings.

N.B. *Ubediti* and *zadržati se* are perfective verbs, their imperfective equivalents are *ubedjivati* (Cl. 4b) and *zadržavati se* (Cl. 5).

Sleteti (to land) is also a perfective sixth-class verb, but its imperfective equivalent *sletati* that appears in the dialogue is conjugated as a 2b class verbs (*slećem* . . .).

Present tense stem

Apart from the infinitive stem that is derived by dropping the infinitive ending -*ti*, all verbs also have a present tense stem.

The present tense stem is derived by dropping the ending -*mo* from the first-person plural in the present tense (*ide-mo, piše-mo, putuje-mo*). The table below gives the six classes of verbs, their infinitive stem, present tense stem, and first-person singular and third-person plural forms:

Cl.	*verb*	*inf. stem*	*present stem*	*1st p.sing.*	*3rd p.pl.*
1a	tresti (shake)	tres-	trese-	tresem	tresu
1b	ići (go)	id-	ide-	idem	idu
1c	jesti (eat)	jed-	jede-	jedem	jedu
2a	zvati (call)	zva-	zove-	zovem	zovu
2b	pisati (write)	pisa-	piše-	pišem	piše
3	krenuti (come)	krenu-	krene-	krenem	krene

Cl.	verb	inf. stem	present stem	1st p.sing.	3rd p.pl.
4a	piti (drink)	pi-	pije-	pijem	piju
4b	putovati (travel)	putova-	putuje-	putujem	putuju
5	čekati (wait)	čeka-	čeka-	čekam	čekaju
6a	raditi (work)	radi-	radi-	radim	rade
6b	živeti (live)	žive-	živi-	živim	žive
6c	držati (hold)	drža-	drži-	držim	drže

Although some verbs have identical infinitive and present tense stems, the two kinds of stems have different functions and should not be confused. The infinitive stem is used for building the short form of the future tense, a past tense known as "aorist," and the active past participle (which is used for building the past tense, as explained below).

The present tense stem is used for building the present tense, the imperative, and several more complicated grammatical structures (such as the passive voice, which will not be discussed in this book).

The present tense consists of: the present stem + the personal endings. Personal endings for the present tense for all classes of verbs are:

	singular	plural
1st p.	-m	-mo
2nd p.	-š	-te
3rd p.	—	-u (Cl. 1–4)
		-ju (Cl. 5)
		-e (Cl. 6)

The imperative

The imperative is used for initiating an action, expressing a wish or giving instructions and commands. Therefore it only appears in the second-person singular and plural and in the first-person plural.

Vežite se. Put your seat belts on. (lit.: Tie yourselves.)
Predjite na "ti." Start saying *ti*. (lit.: Go onto (saying) *ti*.)
Prodjite. Go through.

The imperative is formed by dropping the third-person plural ending of the present tense and adding the imperative ending. Thus:

vež-u, predj-u, prodj-u

vež-
predj-   + the imperative endings
prodj-

The stem derived by dropping the third-person plural ending of the present tense has been referred to as the present tense stem. Although the two stems sometimes coincide, the stem used for building the imperative can be different from the present tense stem.

There are two types of imperative endings, depending on the ending of the derived stem. Fourth and fifth-class verbs (*piti*, *putovati*, and *čekati*) have a stem that ends in *j* and therefore take type 1 endings:

2nd person singular: *-j* (*putuj*)
1st person plural: *-jmo* (*putujmo*)
2nd person plural: *-jte* (*putujte*)

All other verbs have type 2 endings:

2nd person singular: *-i* (*idi*)
1st person plural: *-imo* (*idimo*)
2nd person plural: *-ite* (*idite*)

The imperative for the third person is expressed by using the word *neka* in front of the third-person singular or plural present tense form of the verb:

neka putuje let him/her/it travel   *neka putuju* let them travel
neka ide let him/her/it go   *naka idu* let them go

N.B. In the dialogue, the first-person plural of the present tense of the verb *ići* (*idemo*) is used instead of the imperative to express a wish or command. This is an exception.

Wishes or commands can also sometimes be expressed using the conjunction *da* with the present tense of the verb:

da krenemo let's set off! (let's go!)
da vidimo let's see!

The verb *nemoj* "do not"

Nemoj means "do not," "don't," and is an incomplete verb that only takes the imperative form. It is used with other verbs to indicate negative command:

2nd person singular: nemoj
1st person plural: nemojmo
2nd person plural: nemojte

Nemojte mi persirati. Don't address me formally.

Nmoj is often used with the infinitive of other verbs (as in the example above). Alternatively, it can be used with the conjunction *da* and an inflected verb: *Nemojte da mi persirate.*

Active past participle

The active past participle is derived from a verb but resembles an adjective (it agrees with the subject in gender and number). It is used for forming the past tense. The active past participle itself is formed by adding relevant endings to the infinitive stem of the verb. If the infinitive stem ends in a vowel, the endings are:

masculine singular: *-o*   masculine plural: *-li*
feminine singular: *-la*   feminine plural: *-le*
neuter singular: *-lo*   neuter plural: *-la*

If the infinitive stem ends in a consonant, the masculine singular ending is *-ao*. The endings for all other genders and numbers are the same as above.

Examples of active past participles:

	sing.	*pl.*	*sing.*	*pl.*	*sing.*	*pl.*
masc.:	pisao	pisali	vezao	vezali	krenuo	krenuli
fem.:	pisala	pisale	vezala	vezale	krenula	krenule
neut.:	pisalo	pisala	vezalo	vezala	krenulo	krenula
masc.:	putovao	putovali	morao	morali	video	videli
fem.:	putovala	putovale	morala	morale	videla	videle
neut.:	putovalo	putovala	moralo	morala	videlo	videla

First-class verbs have irregular active past participles, because they have particular infinitive stems. The past participles of *sesti*, *ići*, and *pomoći* are:

	sing.	*pl.*	*sing.*	*pl.*	*sing.*	*pl.*
masc.:	seo	seli	išao	išli	pomogao	pomogli
fem.:	sela	sele	išla	išle	pomogla	pomogle
neut.:	selo	sela	išlo	išla	pomoglo	pomogla

The past tense

The past tense is made with the active past participle and the present tense of the auxiliary verb *biti* (*jesam*). Word order varies in accordance with whether or not the subject is mentioned. The auxiliary verb and the active past participle always agree with the subject in person and number.

Robert je otišao po kolica. Robert went after a baggage cart. (. . . to pick up a baggage cart.)
Hteo je da vidi Beograd. He wanted to see Belgrade.
Kako ste putovali? How did you travel? (Did you have a good journey?)
Videli su Beograd. They saw Belgrade.

N.B. The short forms of the auxiliary *jesam* are used in the affirmative only.

The past tense can be translated in English as either the simple past or the present perfect, depending on context.

Past tense of reflexive *nadati se* "to hope"

nadao (-la,-lo) sam se (I hoped)   nadali (-le,-la) smo se (we hoped)
nadao si se (you hoped)   nadali ste se (you *pl.* hoped)
nadao se (he/she/it hoped)   nadali su se (they hoped)

Notice that in the third-person singular past tense form, reflexive verbs do not require the auxiliary verb (the form *je* is dropped).

If the subject is stated, word order changes:

Ja sam se nadao   Mi smo se nadali
Ti si se nadao   Vi ste se nadali
On se nadao   Oni su se nadali

The interrogative past tense

The interrogative in the past tense can be formed in two ways:

* By using the relevant inflection of the long form of the auxiliary *jesam*, followed by the interrogative particle *li*, followed by the active past participle:

  Jesmo li sleteli? Have we landed yet?
  Jeste li našli svoj prtljag? Have you found your luggage?

* By using the question marker *da li* followed by the relevant short form of the auxiliary *jesam* followed by the active past participle:

  Da li smo sleteli? Have we landed yet?
  Da li ste našli svoj prtljag? Have you found your luggage?

Of course, questions can also be formed using the interrogative pronouns, where the interrogative pronoun is followed by the auxiliary verb followed by the active past participle:

Kako ste putovali?
(lit.: How did you travel?) Did you have a good journey?

A more complicated example from the dialogue includes:

Koliko dugo niste bili u Beogradu?
How long have you not been in Belgrade?
(meaning: When was the last time you were in Belgrade?)

This particular interrogative form uses the interrogative pronoun *koliko dugo* (how long) followed by a negative statement in the past tense.

The negative past tense

The negative past tense is built using the negative present tense forms of the auxiliary "to be"—*nisam* followed by the active past participle of the relevant verb.

Nisam bio u Beogradu dve godine. I haven't been to Belgrade for two years.
Ona nije imala problema na aerodromu. She didn't have problems at the airport.
Nisu hteli da vide moj pasoš. They didn't want to see my passport.

N.B. The subject is often omitted from sentences because it is implied by the inflection of the auxiliary verb and by the inflection of the active past participle.

ADDITIONAL EXPLANATIONS

The possessive dative

Gde su nam pasoši? Where are our passports?

Here the dative form *nam* of the personal pronoun *mi* (we) is used to indicate possession (instead of a possessive pronoun). This use of the "possessive dative" is possible with other personal pronouns, too:

Gde mi je brat? Where is my brother?
Stigao vam je prtljag. Your baggage has arrived.

Oba "both"

Oba is used just as the English "both" to refer inclusively to two objects. *Oba* behaves like the number "two" linguistically in that it takes the genitive singular form of masculine and neuter nouns:

oba pasoša both passports; *oba sela* both villages

The feminine *obe*, like *dve* (two), takes the nominative plural form with feminine nouns:

obe prijateljice both friends

Što as a conjunction

Što functions as a conjunction in several ways. *Što* is most commonly used in response to the question *zašto* (why), in combination with *zato* to form *zato što* (because).

Zadržali su me zato što imam dvojno državljanstvo. They kept me because I have dual citizenship.

USEFUL PHRASES

Vežite se, slećemo.
(VEzhitteh-seh, SLEHchemmoh)
Put your seat belts on, we are about to land.

Ja sam stranac, a ona je strankinja.
(yah-sam STRAAnats, ah onnah-yeh STRANkinnyah)
I am a foreigner, and she is a foreigner.

Molim vas, možete li mi pomoći?
(MOLlim-vass MOZHetteh-lih-mi pomMOTchih)
Please, can you help me?

Gde se čeka prtljag?
(GDEH-seh-CHEKkah PRTlyag)
Where do we wait for the luggage?

Gde mogu da nadjem kolica?
(GDEH-moggoo dah-NAAHdyem kolLEEtza)
Where can I find a baggage cart?

Nemam ništa da prijavim za carinu.
(nemam NISHtah dah-PRIHyavim zah-TZAARinnoo)
I do not have anything to declare (at customs).

Kako ste putovali?
(kakoh-steh PUTtovalih)
Did you have a good journey? (How did you travel?)

Sve je u redu. Nema problema.
(SVEH-yeh u-REHDdu. NEMmah probBLEHmah)
Everything is all right. No problem.

Molim vas predjite na "ti," ne morate da mi persirate.
(MOLlim-vass PREHdyitteh nah-TIH, NEH-moratteh da-mi PERSsirratte).
Please go onto (start saying) *ti*, you don't have to address me formally.

Važi.
(VAAHzhih)
OK.

Svakako.
(SVAKkakoh)
By all means.

EXERCISES

I. Answer the questions with complete sentences.

1. Koliko dugo Marko nije bio u Jugoslaviji?
2. Je li Robert stranac?
3. Je li Jelena strankinja?
4. Sa kim Jelena čeka prtljag?
5. A gde je Robert?
6. Zašto su Marka zadržali na pasoškoj kontroli?
7. Šta Robert ima da prijavi za carinu?
8. Šta Marko ima da prijavi za carinu?
9. Kako se zove Jelenin brat?
10. Koga je Marko upoznao na aerodromu?

II. Put the following statements into the past tense.

1. Avion sleće.
2. Nadamo se.
3. Prolazite.
4. Robert misli da je sve u redu.
5. Vidim Beograd.
6. Jelena pije kafu.
7. Jelena, Robert i Marko čekaju.
8. Robert upoznaje Vladu i Marka.

III. Put the same statements into the interrogative and negative past tense forms.

IV. Put the following verbs into all inflections of the imperative.

sesti
pisati
znati
nadati se

naći
leteti
upoznati

V. Decline the following possessive pronouns and nouns through all cases.

vaš pasoš
moja torba
tvoja godina

LESSON
SEVEN

DIALOGUE

U hotelu

JELENA:	Dakle, vidimo se večeras. Ako bude problema, javi nam se. Imaš našu adresu i broj telefona.
MARKO:	Da. Hvala vam puno.
ROBERT:	Treba li ti pomoć sa stvarima?
MARKO:	Ne, ne treba, hvala. Mogu sam.
JELENA:	Da te bar otpratimo do recepcije. Hajdemo.

RECEPCIONAR:	Dobar dan, izvolite?
MARKO:	Treba mi jedna soba za večeras.
RECEPCIONAR:	Želite li jednokrevetnu ili dvokrevetnu sobu?
MARKO:	Jednokrevetnu. Sa kupatilom.
RECEPCIONAR:	Sve naše sobe su sa kupatilom. Ostajete samo jednu noć?

MARKO:	Da.
RECEPCIONAR:	Vaše ime i prezime, molim?
MARKO:	Marko Petrović.
RECEPCIONAR:	Mogu li da vidim vaš pasoš?
MARKO:	Naravno. U koliko sati služite doručak?
RECEPCIONAR:	Od sedam do deset u malom restoranu. Izvolite ovo je vaš ključ, soba šesto jedanaest.

At the Hotel

JELENA: So, we'll see each other tonight. If there are any problems, you have our address and telephone number.

MARKO: Yes. Thank you very much.

ROBERT: Do you need help with the luggage?

MARKO: No, I don't, thank you. I can take it on my own.

JELENA: Let us at least walk you to the lobby (reception desk). Let's go.

RECEPTIONIST: Good afternoon, how can I help you?

MARKO: I need a room for tonight.

RECEPTIONIST: Do you need a single or a double room?

MARKO: A single room. With a bathroom.

RECEPTIONIST: All our rooms are en suite (with bathroom). You are staying only one night?

MARKO: Yes.

RECEPTIONIST: Can I have your full name, please?

MARKO: Marko Petrović.

RECEPTIONIST: Can I see your passport?

MARKO: Of course. At what time do you serve breakfast?

RECEPTIONIST: From seven to nine in the small restaurant. Here you are, this is your key, room 611.

Marko:	Treba li sada da platim?
Recepcionar:	Možete sutra da platite. Žao mi je, trenutno ne primamo karticu, može samo u gotovini.
Marko:	Nema problema.
Recepcionar:	Sačekajte tu, molim vas, pozvaću vam portira.
Jelena:	Jesi li ga pitao kad ti polazi autobus za aerodrom odavde?
Marko:	Nisam.
Robert:	Bolje pitaj.
Jelena:	Da, evo gospodje iz predstavništva JAT-a. Pitaj nju.
Vlada:	Najbolje da pita na JAT-ovom šalteru.
Marko:	A gde je taj šalter?
Vlada:	Kad izadjete iz hotela skrenete levo u jedan pasaž, nastavite pravo i JAT-ova recepcija je na desnoj strani u pasažu.
Jelena:	Koje im je radno vreme? Sada je već pet sati, sve se zatvara u tri.
Vlada:	Ja mislim da oni rade do osam. Tamo možete i da promenite novac.
Jelena:	Po kom kursu?
Vlada:	Po zvaničnom kursu. Do skoro su svi menjali novac na ulici—kod dilera—jer je zvanični kurs bio mnogo gori od uličnog. Sada je zvanični kurs dobar, ali ako nameravate da menjate novac na ulici, budite vrlo pažljivi.
Robert:	Lepo ga ti savetuješ, Vlado!

MARKO:	Do I need to pay now?
RECEPTIONIST:	You can pay tomorrow. I am sorry, we do not take (credit) cards at the moment, only payment in cash is possible.
MARKO:	No problem.
RECEPTIONIST:	Please, stay here for a moment, I'll call you a porter.
JELENA:	Did you ask him what time your bus for the airport leaves from here?
MARKO:	I didn't.
ROBERT:	You'd better ask.
JELENA:	Yes, there's a lady from the JAT agency. Ask her.
VLADA:	It's best to ask at the JAT counter.
MARKO:	And where is that counter?
VLADA:	When you come out of the hotel you turn left into a passageway, continue straight, and the JAT counter (reception desk) is on the right in the passageway.
JELENA:	What are their opening hours? It's already five o'clock, everything closes at three.
VLADA:	I think they are open until eight. You can change your money there too.
JELENA:	At what exchange rate?
VLADA:	At the official exchange rate. Until recently everybody was changing money on the street—with the dealers— because the official exchange rate was much worse than the black market rate. Now the official exchange rate is good, but if you intend to change the money on the street, be very careful.
ROBERT:	You give (him) really good advice, Vlada!

VOCABULARY

adresa	address
ako	if
ali	but
bar	at least
bolje	better
broj telefona	telephone number
budite (imperative, 2.p.pl)	be!
dakle	so, therefore
desni,-a,-o	right
do	to, until
doručak	breakfast
do skoro	until recently
dvokrevetna soba	a double room (lit.: a two-bed room)
gori	worse
hajdemo	let's go
ime (neut.; nom.pl.: imena)	name
iz	from
izaći (Cl. 1)	to come out, to go out
JAT	(Yugoslav Air transport)
javiti (se) (Cl. 6)	to inform, to get in touch
jednokrevetna soba	a single room (lit.: a one-bed room)
kad	when
(kreditna) kartica	credit card
ključ	key
koji,-a,-e	which, what
kupatilo (neut.)	bathroom
kurs	exchange rate
levi,-a,-o	left
mali,-a,-o	small
menjati (Cl. 5)	to change
mnogo	much
može	it is possible

na	on
najbolje	best
nameravati (Cl. 5)	to intend
naravno	of course
nastaviti (Cl. 6)	to continue
novac	money
od	from
odavde	from here
otpratiti (Cl. 6)	to see sbd off, to walk sbd somewhere
pasaž	passage, open corridor, arcade
pažljiv,-a,-o	careful
pitati (Cl. 5)	to ask
platiti (Cl. 6)	to pay
po	in, after, for
polaziti (Cl. 6)	to depart, to leave, to set off
pomoć (fem.)	help
portir	porter
pozvati (Cl. 2)	to call up
pravo	straight
predstavništvo	office, agency
prezime (neut.)	surname
(nom. pl.: prezimena)	
primati (Cl. 5)	to receive
promeniti	change, exchange
radno vreme	working time, opening hours
recepcija	reception
restoran	restaurant
sačekati (Cl. 5)	to wait for a while
sada	now
sam,-a,-o	alone, on one's own
samo	only
savetovati (Cl. 4)	to advise, to give advice
skrenuti (Cl. 3)	to turn
služiti (Cl. 6)	to serve
soba	room
strana	side
sutra	tomorrow
svi	all, everybody

šalter	counter, point
taj, ta, to	that
tamo	over there
telefon	telephone
treba	it is necessary, it is needed
trenutno	at the moment
tu	there/here
u gotovini	in cash
ulica	street
ulični,-a,-o (adj.)	street
već	already
vrlo	very
za	for
zatvoren,-a,-o	closed
zatvoriti (Cl. 5)	to close
zvanični,-a,-o	official

EXPLANATIONS

Asking for directions

There are several ways of asking for directions, depending on the situation:

Izvinite, možete li mi reći kako da dodjem do (name of place in the genitive)*?*
Excuse me, could you tell me how to get to . . .?

Izvinite, gde se nalazi (name of place in the nominative)*?*
Excuse me where is . . .?

Gde je ovde (name of place in the nominative)*?*
Where is . . . around here?

Je li ovo put za (name of place in the accusative)*?*
Is this the road to . . .?

Directions can also be given in a variety of ways. The key words to remember are:

pravo straight
levo left
desno right
napred forward
nazad back
skrenuti to turn
vratiti se to turn back
nastaviti to continue
sleva to the left
zdesna to the right
levo / desno od . . . to the left / right of . . .
na levoj strani ulice on the left-hand side of the street
na desnoj strani ulice on the right-hand side of the street

Distance is expressed in meters.

Street names

Streets often bear the name of an important person, famous place or historical event. Street names therefore often take the form of a possessive adjective. (Possessive adjectives were discussed in Lesson Five.) The noun *ulica* (street-pronounced: OOLlitsa) is a feminine noun, therefore street names often appear in the form of a feminine adjective:

Knez Mihailova (ulica) Knez Mihailova (Street)*
Sarajevska (ulica) Sarajevska (Street)**

Ulica (street) is often left out when naming the street. If mentioned, the word *ulica* follows the street name, and is spelled in lowercase:

Britanska čitaonica je u Knez Mihailovoj ulici. The British Library is in Knez Mihailova street.

Street names in the form of possessive adjectives are also declined, following the same declension pattern as other adjectives.

Street names can appear in the genitive case:

(Ulica) Džordža Vašingtona the Street of George Washington
(Ulica) Kneza Miloša the Street of Knez Miloš

Here, obviously, the word *ulica* precedes the name of the street:

On živi u (Ulici) Kneza Miloša. He lives in Kneza Miloša (Street).

In this example, the word *ulica*, if used, is declined, whereas the name of the street always stays in the genitive form. If the word *ulica* is given, it is spelled with a capital letter as in the example above.

Knez Mihailova ulica—the most famous pedestrian street in Belgrade—is named after Prince Mihailo Obrenović. The word *knez* means "prince." The literal translation of the street name is: Prince Mihailo's (Street)."
**Sarajevska is obviously named after the city of Sarajevo. The ending *-ska* can be used for turning nouns into adjectives. Such adjectives are discussed in Lesson Eight.

During the socialist years, streets were often named after an important date from the Second World War. In the past ten years, many of the street names inspired by the socialist revolution have been changed back to their pre-Second World War names. It is still possible to come across examples such as:

(Ulica) 29 Novembra.

Again in this example, the name of the street is in the genitive form—"dvadeset devetog novembra"—and isn't declined any further.

Most towns are likely to have squares and boulevards. The word for square is *trg*, which is a masculine noun, as is *bulevar* (boulevard). The names of squares can also appear as adjectives (and are declined like other adjectives):

Cvetni trg the Flowers' Square
Studentski trg the Students' Square

Or more frequently in the genitive form:

Trg slobode the Square of Freedom

In the latter example, the word *trg* is declined like all masculine nouns, and the name of the square stays in the genitive case.

Similarly, names of boulevards are often given in the genitive and only the word *bulevar* is declined:

Bulevar umetnosti the Boulevard of Arts

Addresses are usually given continental-style, whereby the house number follows the name of the street.

On živi u (Ulici) Kneza Miloša (broj) 60. He lives in the Kneza Miloša (Street) (number) 60.

The words in parentheses can be used but are not absolutely necessary.

GRAMMAR

Declension of the personal pronouns "he," "she," "it," and "they"

As we have seen before, personal pronouns have their own declension. The declensions of the first person singular and plural (*ja*, *mi*), and the second person singular and plural (*ti*, *vi*) pronouns were presented in Lesson Five. The declension of the third person singular and plural is presented here:

	singular			*plural*		
	masc.	*neut.*	*fem.*	*masc.*	*neut.*	*fem.*
Nom.:	on	ono	ona	oni	ona	one
Gen.:	njega/ga	"	nje/je	njih/ih	"	"
Dat.:	njemu/mu	"	njoj/joj	njima/im	"	"
Acc.:	njega/ga	"	nju/je/ju	njih/ih	"	"
Voc.:	—	—	—	—	—	—
Instr.:	njim(e)	"	njom(e)	njima	"	"
Prep.:	njemu	"	njoj	njima	"	"

Except for the nominative case, the singular forms of masculine and neuter nouns are the same in most cases as are the plural forms of all three genders. Some cases have a longer and a shorter form which are used variably depending on context. The shorter form is more commonly used. The longer form is used when the emphasis of the sentence is on the object represented by the pronoun.

Interrogative pronoun *koji, koja, koje* "which"

The declension of the interrogative pronoun *koji,-a,-e* (which) is equivalent to the declension of the possessive pronouns *moj, tvoj, naš*, and *vaš* presented in Lesson Six.

Demonstrative pronoun *taj, ta, to* "that"

The demonstrative pronoun *taj* (that) is also declined similarly to other pronouns:

	singular			plural		
	masc.	*neut.*	*fem.*	*masc.*	*neut.*	*fem.*
Nom.:	taj	to	ta	ti	ta	te
Gen.:	tog(a)	"	te	tih	"	tih
Dat.:	tom(e)	"	toj	tim(a)	"	tim
Acc.:	taj/tog(a)*	to	tu	te	ta	te
Voc.:	—	—	—	—	—	—
Instr.:	tim	"	tom	tim(a)	"	tim
Prep.:	tom(e)	"	toj	tim(a)	"	tim

*The accusative singular form of the masculine pronoun is equivalent to its nominative singular form when the pronoun refers to an inanimate object:

Koji sok želite? Which juice do you want?
Želim taj sok. I want that juice.

It is equivalent to the genitive singular form when referring to a living being:

Kojeg prijatelja ste videli? Which friend did you see?
Video sam tog prijatelja. I saw that friend.

The declension of the demonstrative pronoun *ovaj, ova, ovo* (pl.: *ovi, ove, ova*) "which," is equivalent to the declension of *taj*.

Declension of adjectives

In Lesson Four we reviewed some of the cases of the number one, which is declined as an adjective (since it can function as an adjective). (Its plural nominative forms are *jedni, jedne, jedna* for masculine, feminine, and neuter gender respectively.)

Here we shall examine the declension of the definite adjective *mali* (small).
The declension of indefinite adjectives is almost identical—the exceptions
are a matter of linguistic propriety. The model below is widely used in
everyday register.

	singular			*plural*		
	masc.	*neut.*	*fem.*	*masc.*	*neut.*	*fem.*
Nom.:	mali	malo	mala	mali	mala	male
Gen.:	malog(a)	"	male	malih	"	"
Dat.:	malom	"	maloj	malim(a)	"	"
Acc.:	mali/malog*	malo	malu	male	"	"
Voc.:	mali!	malo!	mala!	mali!	mala!	male!
Instr.:	malim	"	malom	malim(a)	"	"
Prep.:	malom	maloj	"	malim(a)	"	"

*The accusative singular form of the masculine adjective is equivalent to its
nominative singular form if the noun it accompanies denotes an inanimate
object:

Vidim mali kofer. I see a small suitcase.

If the masculine adjective accompanies a noun that denotes a living being,
its accusative singular form is equivalent to its genitive singular form:

Vidim malog čoveka. I see a small man.

Comparison of adjectives

There are three degrees in the comparison of adjectives:

1) the positive (equality): "as . . . as"—the basic adjective, such as *srećan,*
   -a,-o (happy)
2) the comparative (relative superiority): "more . . ."—which denotes a
   characteristic of a higher degree than the one denoted by the positive
3) the superlative (absolute superiority): "the most . . ."—which denotes a
   characteristic of the highest degree

The comparative is formed by adding the relevant ending to the base of the adjective.

• Most adjectives take the ending *-iji,-a,-e*:

srećan: srećn + iji (+ ija, + ije)
hladan: hladn + iji (+ ija, + ije)

Notice the fleeting "a" in the base of the adjective.

• Some adjectives take the ending *-ji,-a,-e*. The *j* in the ending then causes a phonetic and morphological change in the base of the adjective.

crn (black): crn + ji (+ ja, + je) = crnji,-a,-e
sladak (sweet): slad + ji (+ ja, + je) = sladji,-a,-e

N.B. Some polysyllabic adjectives lose the final syllable to form the base, for example *slad-ak*.

• There are only three adjectives in Serbo-Croat that form the comparative with the ending *-ši,-a,-e*:

lep,-a,-o (beautiful)	*lepši,-a,-e* (more beautiful)
lak,-a,-o (light)	*lakši,-a,-e* (lighter)
mek,-a,-o (soft)	*mekši,-a,-e* (softer)

• There are four adjectives in Serbo-Croat that have an irregular comparative form. Their comparatives are not derived directly from their positives:

dobar,-a,-o (good)	*bolji,-a,-e* (better)
loš,-a,-e (bad)	*gori,-a,-e* (worse)
mali,-a,-o (small)	*manji,-a,-e* (smaller)
velik,-a,-o (big)	*veći,-a,-e* (bigger)

The superlative is formed by adding the prefix *naj-* to the comparative form of the adjective (both regular and irregular):

najsrećniji,-a,-e (the happiest)
najlepši,-a,-e (the most beautiful)

najsladji,-a,-e (the sweetest)
najbolji,-a,-e (the best)

Both the comparative and the superlative forms are declined like definite adjectives. The comparative and the superlative in the neuter gender can sometimes function as adverbs.

Adverbs

Adverbs are invariable words that have no declension. They can be divided into several categories based on which word they modify and their function in the sentence. There are adverbs that accompany verbs, and adverbs that accompany other adverbs and adjectives.

Adverbs that accompany verbs:

adverbs for place: *ovde* (here), *tu* (here/there), *tamo* (over there), *odavde* (from here), *gde* (where), *gore* (up), *dole* (down), *pravo* (straight), *levo* (left), *desno* (right), *blizu* (near), *daleko* (far), etc.

adverbs for time: *juče* (yesterday), *danas* (today), *sutra* (tomorrow), *ujutru* (in the morning), *uveče* (in the evening), *kada* (when), *sada* (now), *trenutno* (at the moment), *već* (already), etc.

adverbs for manner: *dobro* (well), *lepo* (nicely), *kako* (how), *brzo* (quickly), etc.

adverbs for cause: *zato* (because), *stoga* (therefore), etc.

adverbs for quantity: *malo* (little), *mnogo* (much), *još* (more), *dosta* (enough), etc.

Adverbs that accompany adjectives or other adverbs refer to the degree of a particular characteristic expressed by them, such as *vrlo* (very):

Ona je vrlo lepa. She is very beautiful.
Vrlo lepo pevate. You sing very nicely.

Biti "to be" (present, future, past, imperative)

We have already studied *jesam*, an incomplete auxiliary verb that is used in the present tense only and corresponds to the present tense of the verb *biti* (to be).

The verb *biti* (to be) also has its own present tense conjugation that does not have the same meaning as *jesam* and cannot be used for the same function. Instead it is used as an auxiliary verb to build more complex grammatical structures.

biti (to be)

present tense

budem	budemo
budeš	budete
bude	budu

future tense

biću	bićemo
bićeš	bićete
biće	biće

past tense

bio (bila, bilo) sam	bili (bile, bila) smo
bio,-la,-lo si	bili,-le,-la ste
bio,-la,-lo je	bili,-le,-la su

imperative

—	budimo
budi	budite
(neka) bude	(neka) budu

The present tense of *biti* is often used to imply the future (or to build more complex grammatical tenses). Here is an example from the dialogue:

Ako bude problema, javi nam se. If there are problems, let us know.

Impersonal use of verbs

Some verbs can be used "impersonally," without a subject in the sentence. The verb is always in the third-person singular form. An aforementioned example is the impersonal use of the verb *imati* (to have), which then acquires the meaning "to exist":

Ima li ovde dobrih hotela? Are there any good hotels around here?

An example from the dialogue:

Može samo u gotovini. It is possible (to pay) only in cash.

Other examples:

Biće kiše. It will be raining.
Ako bude problema, javite se. If there are problems, get in touch.

The verb *treba* "is needed, should"

The verb *treba* is an incomplete verb that is only used impersonally. It means "it is necessary," "it is needed." *Treba* is often accompanied by the dative case of the subject.

Treba li vam pomoć? Do you need any help?
Treba mi soba za večeras. I need a room for tonight.
Marku treba soba za večeras. Marko needs a room for tonight.

Treba also has the meaning of "should":

Treba da se javimo Marku. We should get in touch with Marko.

The third-person plural form is used if the necessity applies to a plural object:

Trebaju mi dve sobe za večeras. I need two rooms for tonight.

Future:

Trebaće mi jedna soba. I will need one room.

Past:

Trebala mi je jedna soba. I needed one room.
Trebao mi je taksi. I needed a taxi.
Trebalo mi je vaše ime i prezime. I needed your name and surname.

N.B. Other inflections of the verb do exist grammatically, but are only used in Croatian:

	singular	*plural*
1st p.	trebam	trebamo
2nd p.	trebaš	trebate
3rd p.	treba	trebaju

USEFUL PHRASES

Ako bude problema javite mi se.
(akkoh-BOODdeh probBLEHmah YAAHvitteh-mee seh)
If there are any problems, please call me.

- *Treba li vam pomoć sa stvarima?*
  (TREBbah-lee-vam POMmoch sah-STVAARrimmah)
  Do you need any help with your luggage?
- *Ne treba, hvala, mogu sam/a.*
  (NEHtrebba, khvalah, MOGgoo saam/ah)
  I don't, thanks, I can manage it myself.

Treba mi jednokrevetna soba sa kupatilom za večeras.
(TREBbah-mee YEDdnoh-KREVvetnah SOBbah sah KUPpatillom zah-
    vetCHErass)
I need a single en suite room for tonight.

U koliko sati služite doručak?
(oo-kolLIKkoh SAAtih SLOOzhitteh DORruchak)
What time do you serve breakfast?

Treba li sada da platim? Da li primate karticu?
(TREBbah-lih SADdah-dah PLAAtim. dah-lih PREEmatteh KAARtitzu)
Do I need to pay now? Do you accept credit cards?

Možete li mi pozvati portira?
(MOHzhetteh-lih-mih POZzvatih porTEErah)
Can you call me a porter, please?

Možete li mi reći gde je JAT-ov šalter?
(MOHzhetteh-lih-mih RETchih gde-ye YATtov SHAAHLterr)
Can you tell me where JAT's counter is?

Koje je vaše radno vreme?
(KOYyeh-yeh VASHeh RAADdnoh VREHmeh)
What are your working (opening) hours?

Možete li me posavetovati gde da promenim novac?
(MOHzhetteh-lih-me posSAAHvetovvati GDEH-dah PROMmennim NOV-
vatz)
Can you give me some advice as to where to change my money?

Po kom kursu menjate novac?
(po-KOMM KOORsu MEINyateh NOVvatz)
At what exchange rate do you change money?

EXERCISES

I. Replace the personal names with the correct case of the personal pronoun.

 1. Ako bude problema, Marko će se javiti Robertu i Jeleni.
 2. Marku ne treba pomoć sa stvarima.
 3. Vlada lepo savetuje Marka.
 4. Marko će se videti sa Robertom i Jelenom večeras.

II. Create as many questions as possible from the statements below, using the interrogative pronouns *ko*, *šta*, *koliko*, *gde*, *kada*, *zašto*, and *koji* in the relevant case:

 1. Marko će se javiti Robertu i Jeleni.
 2. Marku treba jedna soba za večeras.
 3. Hotel "Slavija" trenutno ne prima kreditnu karticu.
 4. JAT-ov šalter je na desnoj strani u pasažu.
 5. Marko će promeniti novac po zvaničnom kursu.
 6. Marko će se videti sa Robertom i Jelenom večeras u Skadarliji.
 7. Marko je srećan zato što će se videti sa njima večeras.
 8. Marko nije bio u Beogradu dve godine.

III. Conjugate the following verbs in the past, present, and future tenses and in the imperative.

 1. javiti se
 2. služiti
 3. pitati
 4. platiti
 5. skrenuti
 6. nastaviti
 7. nameravati
 8. menjati
 9. savetovati
 10. izaći

IV. Decline the following adjectives and nouns.

   1. jednokrevetna soba
   2. kreditna kartica
   3. veliki restoran
   4. radno vreme*

(*vreme—nom. pl.: vremena; gen. sing.: vremena; gen. pl.: vremena, etc.)

LESSON
EIGHT

DIALOGUE

U Restoranu

MARKO: Baš je lepo ovde. Svež vazduh, muzika, prijatna atmosfera.

JELENA: Zar ti nikad nisi bio ovde?

MARKO: Ne, jer nikada nisam imao prilike, uvek žurim negde.

ROBERT: Je li ovde dozvoljeno pušenje? Ne vidim pepeljaru.

JELENA: Mora da je dozvoljeno, u ovoj zemlji svi puše. Pitaćemo konobara.

KONOBAR: Dobro veče, izvolite? Želite li nešto da naručite?

ROBERT: Nismo još pregledali jelovnik. Možete li nešto da nam preporučite?

KONOBAR: "Karadjordjeva šnicla" je naš specijalitet, zatim mešano meso
sa roštilja, ćevapi, pljeskavice, ražnjići . . .

MARKO: Imate li nešto za vegetarijance?

KONOBAR: Gibanicu, proju . . . Razne salate—"urnebes," "šopsku" . . . Da
li jedete ribu?

MARKO: Ako baš moram.

KONOBAR: Imamo razne vrste sveže ribe.

JELENA: Ja bih jednu "Karadjordjevu šniclu."

ROBERT: I ja.

MARKO: A ja bih porciju lignji sa krompirom, i donesite nam nekoliko
vrsta salata.

At the Restaurant

MARKO: It's very nice here. Fresh air, music, nice atmosphere.

JELENA: Have you never been here before?

MARKO: No, I never had a chance, always rushing somewhere.

ROBERT: Is smoking allowed in here? I don't see an ashtray.

JELENA: It must be (allowed), everybody smokes in this country. We'll
           ask the waiter.

WAITER: Good evening, what would you like? Would you like to order
           anything?

ROBERT: We haven't looked through the menu yet. Can you recommend
           anything?

WAITER: "Karadjordje's cutlet" is our specialty, then mixed barbecued
           meat, "ćevapi," beef burgers, shish kebab . . .

MARKO: Do you have anything vegetarian?

WAITER: "Gibanica," "proja" . . . Various salads—"urnebes," "šopska" . . .
           Do you eat fish?

MARKO: If I really have to.

WAITER: We have various sorts of fresh fish.

JELENA: I'd (like) a "Karadjordje's cutlet."

ROBERT: Me, too.

MARKO: And I'd (like) a portion of squid with some potatoes, and could
           you bring us a few kinds of salad.

KONOBAR: Šta biste želeli da popijete?

ROBERT: Ja bih neko crno vino.

JELENA: A ja belo.

MARKO: I ja. I jednu flašu kisele vode, molim vas.

MARKO: A gde je Vlada večeras?

JELENA: Na treningu. On je košarkaš.

MARKO: I rekao bih po njegovoj visini. Ja više volim fudbal.

KONOBAR: Izvolite, crno i belo vino, kisela voda. Hrana stiže za petnaest minuta.

ROBERT: Izvinite, je li dozvoljeno pušenje ovde?

KONOBAR: Da, naravno. Doneću vam pepeljaru.

ROBERT: A da li znate gde mogu da kupim cigare?

KONOBAR: Ima jedna trafika tu niže malo. Oni rade celu noć.

ROBERT: A izvinite, da li znate koliko otprilike košta jedna kutija?

KONOBAR: Zavisi šta želite. Cene se kreću najviše do tri evra po kutiji.

ROBERT: Hvala. Idem ja da kupim cigare.

JELENA: Pa idi posle večere. I onako pušenje nije dobro za tebe.

MARKO: Baš sam gladan.

JELENA: Uzmi malo hleba dok čekamo. Jesi li se bar malo odmorio?

MARKO: Imaću ja dovoljno vremena za odmor.

ROBERT: Znači ti putuješ nazad krajem meseca?

WAITER: What would you like to drink?

ROBERT: I'd like some red wine.

JELENA: And I'd like some white wine.

MARKO: Me, too. And a bottle of sparkling mineral water, please.

MARKO: And where is Vlada tonight?

JELENA: At a training. He is a basketball player.

MARKO: I'd say so too (judging) by his height. I prefer football.

WAITER: Here you are, red and white wine, sparkling water. The food will be ready in fifteen minutes.

ROBERT: Excuse me, is smoking allowed here?

WAITER: Yes, of course. I'll bring you an ashtray.

ROBERT: And do you know where I can buy some cigarettes?

WAITER: There is a newsstand just down the road. They're open all night.

ROBERT: And do you know roughly how much one pack costs?

WAITER: It depends on what you want. The prices range up to about three Euros per pack.

ROBERT: Thank you. I'm going to buy some cigarettes.

JELENA: Well, go after dinner. Smoking is not good for you anyway.

MARKO: I'm very hungry.

JELENA: Take some bread while we're waiting. Have you had a little rest?

MARKO: I'll have enough time for rest.

ROBERT: So you are traveling back at the end of the month?

MARKO: Da, oko dvadeset osmog juna. Mislim da je to petak.

JELENA: Subota.

MARKO: Da, i onda u ponedeljak na posao!

ROBERT: Jelena, imamo li mi Markovu imejl adresu? I jesmo li mu dali naše?

JELENA: Da, razmenili smo adrese, i svakako ćemo ostati u vezi!

MARKO: A evo i hrane!

* * *

ROBERT: Šteta što ne jedeš meso. Zaista ne znaš šta si propustio.

MARKO: Meni je i moje povrće prijalo! Zaista služe divnu hranu ovde.

JELENA: Jeste li za dezert?

ROBERT: Ne, hvala.

MARKO: I ja sam sit.

JELENA: Da platimo onda?

ROBERT: Da. Konobar, račun molim vas!

MARKO: A, ne, ne, nismo se tako dogovorili. Ja plaćam.

JELENA: Stvarno nema smisla.

MARKO: Vi samo možete da dodate nešto za napojnicu ako imate sitnog novca.

ROBERT: U redu, onda čim se svi vratimo u Njujork, na nas je red!

MARKO: Yes, around the 28th of June. I think that's a Friday.

JELENA: Saturday.

MARKO: Yes, and then on Monday back to work!

ROBERT: Jelena, do we have Marko's email address? And did we give
            him ours?

JELENA: Yes we swapped addresses, we'll stay in touch by all means.

MARKO: And there comes the food.

                                  * * *

ROBERT: It's too bad you don't eat meat. You really don't know what
            you've missed.

MARKO: I've enjoyed my vegetables just as much! They really serve
            wonderful food here.

JELENA: Are you up for a dessert?

ROBERT: No, thanks.

MARKO: I am full, too.

JELENA: Shall we pay then?

ROBERT: Yes. Waiter, the bill please!

MARKO: Oh, no, no, we haven't made such an agreement. I am paying
            the bill.

JELENA: Really, it's not fair.

MARKO: You can only add something for the tip if you have some
            change.

ROBERT: OK then, as soon as we all get back to New York, it's our turn!

VOCABULARY

ako	if
atmosfera	atmosphere
baš	(a particle used for emphasis)
bih	(a present perfect form of the verb "to be"; used to express willingness, "would like")
celi,-a,-o	whole
cena	price
cigare	cigarettes
čim	as soon as
dati	to give
(Cl. 5, dam, daš, da . . .)	
divan,-a,-o	wonderful
dodati	to add
dok	while
doneti	to bring
(Cl. 1, donesem, doneseš, donese . . .)	
dozvoljen,-a,-o	allowed
dvadeset osmi,-a,-o	28th
evro	euro
fudbal	football
gledati (Cl. 5)	to look, to watch
i onako	anyway
jelovnik	menu
jer	because
jun	June
košarkaš	basketball player
koštati (Cl. 5)	to cost
konobar	waiter
kraj	end
krajem	at the end, by the end
kretati se	to move, to range (for prices)
(Cl. 2, krećem se, krećeš se . . .)	
kupiti (Cl. 6)	to buy

kutija	packet
misliti (Cl. 6)	to think
muzika	music
na nas (acc.) je red	it's our turn
napojnica	tip
naručiti (Cl. 6)	to order
nazad	back
negde	somewhere
nekoliko	several
nema smisla	it's not fair (lit.: no meaning)
niže	further down
nikad(a)	never
njegov,-a,-o	his
odmor	rest
odmoriti se (Cl. 6)	to take a rest
oko	around (followed by the genitive)
otprilike	roughly, approximately
pa	(a particle used like "well" or "then")
pepeljara	ashtray
petak	Friday
plaćati (Cl. 5)	to pay
po	after, by, per
ponedeljak	Monday
posao	work
posle	after
pregledati (Cl. 5)	to look through
preporučiti (Cl. 6)	to recommend
prijati	to be pleasant, enjoyable
(mostly used as an impersonal verb, with the dative)	
prilika	chance, opportunity
propustiti (Cl. 6)	to miss
pušenje	smoking
pušiti (Cl. 6)	to smoke
račun	bill
(Cl. 5, dodam, dodaš . . .)	
razmeniti (Cl. 6)	to exchange, to swap
razni,-e,-o	various
(plural only)	

reći (Cl. 1)	to say
sa	from
sitan novac	change (lit.: small money)
stvarno	really
subota	Saturday
svež,-a,-e	fresh
šteta	pity
tako	that way
trafika	newsagent's, newsstand, kiosk
trening	training
urnebes	chaos
uvek	always
uzeti	to take
(Cl.1, uzmem, uzmeš . . .)	
vazduh	air
veza	contact
više	more
visina	height
voleti	to like, to love
(Cl. 6, volim, voliš, voli . . .)	
vratiti se (Cl. 6)	to return
vrsta	kind, sort
za	for, in
(za petnaest minuta: in fifteen minutes)	
zaista	really, indeed
zatim	then
zavisiti (Cl. 6)	to depend
zemlja	country
znači	so, therefore (also: "it means" from *značiti*)
žuriti (Cl. 6)	to hurry, to be in a hurry

Food-related vocabulary

crno vino	red wine (lit.: black wine)
(belo vino: white wine)	
ćevap	rolled finger of minced meat, grilled
dezert	dessert
flaša	bottle
gibanica	a savory cheese pie made with filo-pastry, cottage cheese and eggs
gladan, gladna, gladno	hungry
hleb	bread
hrana	food
jesti	to eat
(Cl 1., jedem, jedeš, jede . . .)	
"Karadjordjeva šnicla"	rolled, breaded veal cutlet, stuffed with cheese
kisela voda	sparkling mineral water (lit.: sour water)
krompir	potato
lignja	squid
mešan,-a,-o	mixed
meso	meat
pljeskavica	(beef) burger
porcija	portion
povrće	vegetables
(coll. neut. n.)	
proja	corn flour (polenta) pastry with cheese and eggs
ražnjić	shish kebab
(mostly in pl.: ražnjići)	
riba	fish
roštilj	barbecue, grill
salata	salad
sit,-a,-o	satiated, full
specijalitet	specialty
šnicla	cutlet
"šopska salata"	tomatoes, raw onions and hot peppers topped with cottage cheese
"urnebes salata"	tomatoes, peppers and cheese with spices made into a paste
vegetarijanac	a vegetarian

EXPLANATIONS

Days of the week

ponedeljak (masc.)	Monday
utorak (masc.)	Tuesday
sreda (fem.)	Wednesday
četvrtak (masc.)	Thursday
petak (masc.)	Friday
subota (fem.)	Saturday
nedelja (fem.)	Sunday

The days of the week (*dani u nedelji*) are declined like all other masculine or feminine nouns.

The names of the days and months are spelled with lowercase letters, unless they appear at the beginning of a sentence. The masculine names (*ponedeljak, utorak, četvrtak, petak*) all feature a fleeting "a" (*ponedeljkom, utorkom,* etc.). Names of days are often preceded by the preposition *u,* the equivalent to "on" in English:

Vraćamo se u utorak. We are returning on Tuesday.
Vidimo se u subotu. See you on Saturday.

N.B. The names of days here are in the accusative case, which affects the ending of the days whose names are in the feminine (*sreda, subota, nedelja*).

The instrumental case is used when expressing a general or habitual action:

Idemo u bioskop utorkom. We go to the cinema on Tuesdays.
Pošta je zatvorena nedeljom. The post office is closed on Sundays.

Similarly day names can appear in the genitive preceded by the adjective
svaki,-a,-e (every), in the genitive also:

Idemo u bioskop svakog utorka. We go to the cinema every Tuesday.
Pošta je zatvorena svake nedelje. The post office is closed every Sunday.

Ordinal numbers

prvi,-a,-o	first
drugi,-a,-o	second
treći,-a,-o	third
četvrti,-a,-o	fourth
peti,-a,-o	fifth
šesti,-a,-o	sixth
sedmi,-a,-o	seventh
osmi,-a,-o	eighth
deveti,-a,-o	ninth
deseti,-a,-o	tenth
jedanaesti,-a,-o	eleventh
dvanaesti,-a,-o	twelfth
trinaesti,-a,-o	thirteenth
četrnaesti,-a,-o	fourteenth
petnaesti,-a,-o	fifteenth
šesnaesti,-a,-o	sixteenth
sedamnaesti,-a,-o	seventeenth
osamnaesti,-a,-o	eighteenth
devetnaesti,-a,-o	nineteenth
dvadeseti,-a,-o	twentieth
dvadeset prvi,-a,-o	twenty-first
dvadeset drugi,-a,-o	twenty-second
trideseti,-a,-o	thirtieth
trideset peti,-a,-o	thirty-fifth
četrdeseti,-a,-o	fortieth
pedeseti,-a,-o	fiftieth
šesdeseti, -a, -o	sixtieth
sedamdeseti,-a,-o	seventieth

osamdeseti,-a,-o	eightieth
devedeseti,-a,-o	ninetieth
stoti,-a,-o	hundredth
dvestoti,-a,-o	two hundredth
tristoti,-a,-o	three hundredth
hiljaditi,-a,-o	one thousandth
hiljadu devetsto pedeset peti,-a,-o	thousand nine hundred fifty-fifth
dve hiljaditi,-a,-o	two thousandth

N.B. Ordinal numbers are declined like adjectives.

Months

Serbian	*Croatian*	
januar	siječanj	January
februar	veljača	February
mart	ožujak	March
april	travanj	April
maj	svibanj	May
jun	lipanj	June
jul	srpanj	July
avgust	kolovoz	August
septembar	rujan	September
oktobar	listopad	October
novembar	studeni	November
decembar	prosinac	December

Dates

Questions relating to specific dates include:

Koji je vaš datum rodjenja? What is your date of birth?

Kog datuma ste rodjeni? On which date were you born?

Kada se vraćate sa odmora? When are you returning from your vacation?

Od kog do kog datuma ne radite? From which to which date are you not working?

Od kada do kada ste na odmoru? From when to when are you on vacation?

Possible answers include:

Rodjen sam prvog juna hiljadu devetsto pedesete godine.* I was born on June 1st, 1950.

Vraćam se u sredu, drugog avgusta. I'm returning on Wednesday, the 2nd of August.

Vraćam se trećeg jula, dve hiljade druge. I'm returning on the 3rd of July 2002.

Ne radim od petog jula do prvog avgusta. I'm not working from July 5 to August 1.

*For a woman the form *rodjena sam* is used. This is the passive voice of the verb *roditi se* (to be born). While the passive voice is not discussed in this book, it is sufficient to memorize this phrase or to use the past tense of the verb instead, as in *Rodio (-la) sam se . . .*

N.B. Names of months are spelled in lowercase unless placed at the beginning of a sentence.

GRAMMAR

Comparative summary of pronouns

Interrogative	*Indefinite*	*Negative*	*Demonstrative*
ko (who)	neko	niko	taj, ovaj, onaj
šta (what)	nešto	ništa	to, ovo, ono
kada (when)	nekada	nikada	tada, onda
gde (where)	negde	nigde	tu, ovde, onde
kako (how)	nekako	nikako	tako, ovako, onako
koliko (how much)	nekoliko	nikoliko	toliko, ovoliko, onoliko
kuda (where)	nekuda	nikuda	tuda, ovuda, onuda

By now you will have encountered the majority of the above pronouns.

Indefinite pronouns generally are derived by adding the prefix *ne-* to the interrogative pronoun and negative pronouns are derived by adding the prefix *ni-* to the interrogative pronoun.

The demonstrative pronoun *ovaj* corresponds with the English "this," *onaj* corresponds with the English "that," and *taj* can mean either "this" or "that." The difference between *taj* and *ovaj* concerns the proximity of the object that is being referred to, *ovaj* being closer than *taj*.

Ovako corresponds with "this way," *onako* corresponds with "that way," and *tako* could mean either; *ovoliko* (this much), *onoliko* (that much), etc.

Declension of the possessive pronouns *njegov,-a,-o* "his" and *njen,-a,-o* "hers"

	singular			plural		
	masc.	*neut.*	*fem.*	*masc.*	*neut.*	*fem.*
Nom.:	njegov	njegovo	njegova	njegovi	njegova	njegove
Gen.:	njegovog(a)	"	njegove	njegovih	"	"
Dat.:	njegovom	"	njegovoj	njegovim(a)	"	"
Acc.:	njegov/(og)	njegovo	njegovu	njegove	njegova	njegove
Voc.:	njegov!	njegovo!	njegova!	njegovi!	njegova!	njegove!
Instr.:	njegovim	"	njegovom	njegovim(a)	"	"
Prep.:	njegovom	"	njegovoj	njegovim(a)	"	"

	singular			plural		
	masc.	*neut.*	*fem.*	*masc.*	*neut.*	*fem.*
Nom.:	njen	njeno	njena	njeni	njena	njene
Gen.:	njenog(a)	"	njene	njenih	"	"
Dat.:	njenom	"	njenoj	njenim(a)	"	"
Acc.:	njen/njenog	njeno	njenu	njene	njena	njene
Voc.:	njen!	njeno!	njena!	njeni!	njena!	njene!
Instr.:	njenim	"	njenom	njenim(a)	"	"
Prep.:	njenom	"	njenoj	njenim(a)	"	"

The possessive pronoun *njihov* (theirs) takes the same case endings as *njegov*.

Possessive adjectives ending in *-ov* (*Markov*), *-ev* (*Djordjev*), and *-in* (*Jelenin*) take the same endings as above, according to gender. (*Markov* and *Djordjev* correspond with *njegov* and *Jelenin* corresponds with *njen*.)

Declension of the adjective *svež,-a,-e* "fresh"

The indefinite adjective *svež,-a,-e* and its definite equivalent *sveži,-a,-e*, ending in the soft consonant *ž*, have a slightly different declension in the singular from other adjectives. For example, the genitive case singular ending is *-eg* rather than *-og* in the masculine and neuter gender, as shown below.

This applies to all adjectives ending in a soft consonant, such as *vruć* (hot), *smedj* (brown), etc.

	singular			*plural*		
	masc.	*neut.*	*fem.*	*masc.*	*neut.*	*fem.*
Nom.:	svež	sveže	sveža	sveži	sveža	sveže
Gen.:	svežeg	"	sveže	svežih	"	"
Dat.:	svežem	"	svežoj	svežim(a)	"	"
Acc.:	svež/(eg)	sveže	svežu	sveže	sveža	sveže
Voc.:	svež!	sveže!	sveža!	sveži!	sveža!	sveže!
Instr.:	svežim	"	svežom	svežim(a)	"	"
Prep.:	svežem	"	svežoj	svežim(a)	"	"

Adjectives ending in -*ski*, -*ški*, -*čki*

Adjectives ending in -*ski*, -*ški*, and -*čki* are definite adjectives that are mostly derived from nouns. Many of these adjectives are derived from nouns referring to geographical names, such as:

engleski jezik (masc.) English language
srpsko jelo (neut.) Serbian dish
praška šunka (fem.) Prague ham
češki jezik (masc.) Czech language
nemačka marka (fem.) German mark
grčko ostrvo (neut) Greek island

Adjectives ending in -*ski*, -*ški*, and -*čki* are declined like other adjectives, where the ending -*i* is replaced by the relevant gender, number and case ending.

N.B. Although derived from nouns spelled with a capital letter, these adjectives are spelled in lowercase, unless appearing at the beginning of the sentence and except in the case of the names of streets—"Sarajevska ulica."

Comparison of the adverb *mnogo* "a lot"

The comparison of adverbs is generally similar to the comparison of adjectives, especially when the adverbs are derived from adjectives. In the case of the adverb *mnogo* (a lot), the comparative and the superlative are substituted by *više* and *najviše* respectively. Therefore:

Robert mnogo voli Beograd. Robert likes Belgrade a lot.
Marko više voli Beograd (od Roberta). Marko likes Belgrade more (than Robert).
Jelena najviše voli Beograd. Jelena likes Belgrade the most.

Please note that the same format is used when expressing preference:

Jelena voli Pariz. Jelena likes Paris.
Jelena više voli Njujork (nego Paris). Jelena prefers New York (to Paris).
Jelena najviše voli Beograd. Jelena likes Belgrade best.

More first-class verbs

Jesti (to eat), *uzeti* (to take), *doneti* (to bring), and *reći* (to say) are all first-class verbs and therefore have a slightly unpredictable conjugation. Their present tense conjugations are given below:

jesti (to eat)

jedem	jedemo
jedeš	jedete
jede	jedu

uzeti (to take)

uzmem	uzmemo
uzmeš	uzmete
uzme	uzmu

doneti (to bring)

donesem	donesemo
doneseš	donesete
donese	donesu

reći (to say)*

reknem	reknemo
rekneš	reknete
rekne	reknu

*Please note that the present tense of *reći* (to say) is very archaic and not normally used. However, other tenses of this verb are used. In the present tense the second-class verb *kazati* (to say, to tell) is more commonly used instead.

Present past tense of *biti* "to be"

In the Serbo-Croatian language there are several past tenses. The past tense discussed in Lesson Seven is called the perfect tense. The imperfect tense is used to express an action that took place before the action referred to by the perfect tense. The pluperfect tense expresses an action even further in the past. The present past tense, also called the aorist verb form, expresses an action that has taken place in the not-too-distant past and is therefore similar to the present past tense in English, although it is not used in the same way. Some of these past tenses, such as the imperfect and the aorist, have an archaic or colloquial quality to them. As these various past tenses are not essential for everyday communication, we shall not explore them in detail in this book.

The aorist forms of *biti* (to be) are used in building the potential—a grammatical form commonly used for expressing possibility, wish or inclination. The aorist forms of "to be" are:

bih	bismo
bi	biste
bi	biše

Although the aorist meaning of "to be" is equivalent to its present past tense meaning, it is rarely used with that purpose. Its significance is in the function of building the potential where it acquires the meaning of the English "would."

The potential

The potential is a grammatical form used for expressing possibility, wish or inclination. It is built with the aorist form of the verb "to be" and the active past participle of the principal verb:

Ja bih popio (-la) jednu kafu. I would like to have a coffee.
    (lit.: I would drink a coffee.)
Ti bi popio (-la) jednu kafu. You would (like to) drink a coffee.
On(a) bi popio (-la) jednu kafu. He/she would like to have a coffee.
Mi bismo popili jednu kafu. We would like to have a coffee.
Vi biste popili jednu kafu. You would like to have a coffee.
Oni bi popili jednu kafu.* They would like to have a coffee.

*Note that for the third-person plural, the third-person singular aorist form of the verb "to be" *bi* is used (and <u>not</u> the third-person plural *biše*).

Of course, the auxiliary verb can also follow the principal verb:

Popio <u>bih</u> jednu kafu. I would like to have a coffee.
Popili <u>bismo</u> jednu kafu. We would like to have a coffee.

N.B. Remember that the active past participle is inflected according to the gender of the subject (see Lesson Six). In the plural the masculine form is used if the subjects are of masculine or mixed gender. If the plural subject is of feminine gender the feminine plural is used:

<u>Popile</u> bismo jednu kafu. We would like to drink a coffee.

The potential is also used for expressing possibility. Depending on context, all of the above examples could be translated as:

Popio bih kafu (i otišao). I would drink a coffee (and leave). – a habitual action.

Popili bi kafu (kad bi imali vremena). They would drink a coffee (if they had the time). – a conditional action.

But it can also imply a possibility in the past (as in the third conditional in English):

Popili bi kafu (da su imali vremena). They would have drunk a coffee (had they had the time).

Impersonal use of *morati* "to have" and *zavisiti* "to depend"

The verbs *morati* (to have) and *zavisiti* (to depend) have a similar impersonal use, as in English where their use becomes idiomatic:

Trava je mokra, mora da je padala kiša. The grass is wet, it must have rained.

Mora da je dozvoljeno (pušenje). It must be allowed (smoking).

A: *Kako se kreću cene cigara?* What is the range of the price of cigarettes?

B: *Zavisi gde kupite.* It depends on where you buy them.

The double negative

Negation in Serbo-Croat is expressed using the double negative if the determiner is used:

Nisam nikada bio u Beogradu. I have never been to Belgrade.

Ne vidim ništa. I don't see anything (lit.: nothing).

Nema nikoga kod kuće. There's (lit.: there isn't) no one at home.

The position of the two negatives in the sentence can be interchanged:

Nikada nisam bio u Beogradu.
Etc.

Other kinds of words

* Copulas

   Copulas are invariable words that are used to connect particular words in a sentence.

   Commonly used copulas include:

   i (and); *ili* (or); *a* (and / but), *ali* (but), *pa* (then), *jer* (because); *da* (to), *ako* (if), etc.

   Copulas also determine the connection between words, for example:

   A and *ali* signify difference or opposition, *jer* signifies a cause, etc.

   Some adverbial pronouns, such as *kako, koji, kada*, etc. can appear as copulas:

   Videćemo se kad dodjete. We'll see each other <u>when</u> you come.

* Particles

   Particles have a particular meaning and function. Often they are adverbs or copulas that are used to express the personal attitude of the agent.

   For particular emphasis: *baš, ala, svakako, naravno*, etc.

Baš je lepo ovde! It's very nice here, indeed.
Ala je lepo ovde! How nice it is here!

For pointing something out: *evo, eto, eno*, etc.

Evo i hrane! There comes the food!

For asking a question: *zar, da li.*

Zar nikada niste bili ovde? Have you never been here before?

* Interjections

   Interjections are particular sounds used to express the moods and feelings of the subject or speaker. Some of these such as "ah!" can signal various moods—joy, pain, frustration, etc.—depending on context. Interjections can be divided generally into:

   Interjections expressing moods: *ah!, uh!, jaoj* ("ouch" or "woe"), *oho!*

   Interjections for calling or deterring animals: *mac* ("kitty"), *iš* (used for deterring hens), etc.

   Onomatopoeic interjections: *dum, tras, bum*, etc.

Question formation with the interrogative particle *zar*

Another way of forming a question in Serbo-Croat is to place the interrogative particle *zar* at the beginning of a sentence followed by a statement:

Zar nikada niste bili ovde? Have you never been here before?

Zar pada kiša? Is it raining?

Zar već? Already?

The interrogative particle *zar* also indicates surprise or wonder.

USEFUL PHRASES

Je li ovde dozvoljeno pušenje?
Mogu li dobiti pepeljaru?
(yeh-li ovdeh DOZzvolyennoh PUSHenyeh)
(MOGgoo-lih DOBbitih pepPELlyaroo)
Is smoking allowed here?
Could I have an ashtray?

Šta želite da naručite?
(shtah-ZHElitteh dah-NARruchitteh)
What would you like to order?

Šta možete da nam preporučite iz jelovnika?
(shtah MOZHetteh dah-nam prepPORruchitteh iz-YELlovnikah)
What can you recommend to us from the menu?

Imate li nešto za vegetarijance?
Ja više volim povrće.
(IMmatteh-lih NESHtoh-za veghetariYANtze)
(yah VISHeh VOLim POVvrcheh)
Do you have anything for vegetarians?
I prefer vegetables.

Da li jedete ribu?
(dah-lih JEDdetteh RIBboo)
Do you eat fish?

Ja bih da probam specijalitet kuće.
(yah-bih-dah PROBbam spetzIYAlitet KOOTcheh)
I'd like to try the speciality of the house.

Da li znate gde mogu da kupim . . .?
(dah-lih ZNATteh gdeh-MOGgoo-da KOOPpim)
Do you know where I can buy . . .?

Gde se prodaje . . .? Koliko košta . . .?
(gdeh-seh PRODdayeh . . . KOHLlikoh KOSHtah)
Where do they sell . . .? How much does . . . cost?

Hoćemo li da razmenimo adrese?
(HOCHemmoh-lih-dah RAZzmennimoh adRESseh)
Shall we exchange addresses?

Baš mi je prijalo.
(bash-mee-yeh PRIYyalloh)
I've really enjoyed it.

Konobar, račun molim vas!
(KONnobar, RACHchun MOLlim-vass)
Waiter, the bill please!

EXERCISES

I.   Answer the questions.

1. Šta je konobar preporučio Robertu, Jeleni i Marku? (in the accusative)
2. Čega ima u restoranu od hrane za vegetarijance?
3. Šta bi Robert i Jelena želeli da pojedu?
4. A šta je Marko naručio?
5. Šta su oni naručili za piće?
6. Zašto Vlada nije sa njima?
7. Koliko košta jedna kutija cigara u Beogradu?
8. Kada se Marko vraća kući?

II. Translate the following sentences into Serbo-Croat.

1. I can't eat any more. I'm really full!
2. How tall are you?
3. When were you born?
4. How much does a flight to Belgrade cost?
5. What can you recommend us to eat?
6. Can you please bring us the bill?
7. Where can I buy fresh vegetables?
8. As soon as I return home, I have to go to work.
9. What do you prefer, tennis or football?
10. Have you already arrived?

III. Conjugate these verbs in the present, past, and future tenses, and in the imperative and the potential.

uzeti
reći*
jesti**

voleti
kretati se
dati

*This verb has an exceptional imperative form: 2nd p. sing.: reci, etc.
**The active past participle of *jesti* is *jeo, jela, jelo*. The singular first person
   in the future tense is *ješću* due to the phonetic change of *s* into *š*. This phonetic alteration applies to all other forms of the verb in the future tense.
   Bear this in mind when doing the exercise.

KEY TO EXERCISES

Pronunciation

1. koka-kola - coca-cola; Amerika - America; fudbal - football;
   1 dolar - 1 dollar; Džordž Vašington - George Washington;
   Mekdonalds - McDonalds; Beograd - Belgrade

2. Njujork - Њујорк; taksi - такси; restoran - ресторан;
   rentakar - рентакар; amerikan ekspres - америкaн експрес;
   London - Лондон

Lesson One

I.
   1. I am an American, and you?
   2. They are French.
   3. This is Jelena. She is a Yugoslav (woman).
   4. We speak Serbian.
   5. Do you speak English?
   6. We are going to the seaside.
   7. Is she going to Belgrade?
   8. What do you do?
   9. Is the stewardess good?
   10. My wife is happy.

II.
   1. Vi ste Francuz.
   2. (Vi) Idete na more.
   3. On je profesor.
   4. (Vi) Govorite francuski.
   5. Deca su dobra.

III.
   1. Je li ovo Jelena?
   2. Je li on Amerikanac?
   3. Jesu li moja deca srećna?
   4. Jesu li moji roditelji Amerikanci?
   5. Je li stjuardesa Jugoslovenka?

IV.
1. Mi smo srećni Amerikanci.
2. On je Francuz, a vi?
3. Ona je Jugoslovenka.
4. Da li oni govore engleski?
5. On govori srpskohrvatski.
6. Ovo je stjuardesa.
   Ona govori engleski.
7. Moja deca su dobra.
8. On ide na more.
9. Mi idemo za (u) Njujork.
10. Idete li vi za (u) Njujork.

Lesson Two

I.
1. Ne, Jelena je Jugoslovenka.
2. Ne, Jelena, je lekar.
3. Da, Marko govori srpskohrvatski.
4. Ne, Marko ide na more.
5. Ne, Robert i Jelena idu u Beograd.
6. Ne, Robert hoće voćni sok.
7. Ne, Jelena želi belu kafu.
8. Ne, Robert želi sok bez leda.

II.
1. Jelena je lekar.
2. Marko je ekonomista.
3. Robert je profesor.
4. Robert je Francuz.
5. Jelena želi jednu belu kafu.
6. Robert hoće sok.
7. Robert, Jelena i Marko govore srpskohrvatski. (Svi govore srpskohrvatski.)

III.
1. Dobar dan, kako ste?
2. Kako se zovete?

3. Robert nije Jugosloven.
4. Jelena hoće (želi) belu kafu bez šećera.
5. Marko želi jedno pivo.
6. Robert pije sok bez leda.
7. Stjuardesa nema sok od pomorandže.
8. Šta (vi) želite da pijete?
9. Ko govori engleski?
10. Imate li kafu?
11. Pijete li pivo?

Lesson Three

I.

1. Marko ide na more. (Marko ide u Budvu.)
2. Robert ide u Beograd na konferenciju.
3. Jelena je iz Beograda.
4. Marko nema direktan let za more.
5. Marko će odsesti u hotelu.

II.

1. Marko ide u Budvu.
2. Moji roditelji su iz Amerike.
3. Marko ima nekoliko prijatelja u Beogradu.
4. Ja imam rodbinu u Kanadi i u Meksiku.
5. Ja želim da ostanem u Beogradu.
6. Ja želim da odsednem u hotelu jednu noć.

III.

	sing.	pl.	sing.	pl.	sing.	pl.
Nom.	hotel	hoteli	tata	tate	mama	mame
Gen.	hotela	hotela	tate	tata	mame	mama
Acc.	hotel	hotele	tatu	tate	mamu	mame
Instr.	hotelom	hotelima	tatom	tatama	mamom	mamama
Prep.	hotelu	hotelima	tati	tatama	mami	mamama

Lesson Four

I.
1. Jelena ostaje u Beogradu mesec dana.
2. Robert ostaje u Beogradu dve nedelje.
3. Marko ostaje na moru deset dana.
4. A u Podgorici (ostaje) nedelju dana.
5. Marko ima prijatelje u Beogradu.
6. Marko ide u Budvu.
7. Marko, Jelena i Robert stižu u petnaest do četiri.
8. Da, oni kasne.
9. Oni kasne petnaest minuta.

II.
Present

sing.	pl.	sing.	pl.	sing.	pl.
popijem	popijemo	kasnim	kasnimo	stajem	stajemo
popiješ	popijete	kasniš	kasnite	staješ	stajete
popije	popiju	kasni	kasne	staje	staju

Future

popiću	popićemo	kasniću	kasnićemo	staću	staćemo
popićeš	popićete	kasnićeš	kasnićete	staćeš	staćete
popiće	popiće	kasniće	kasniće	staće	staće

III.
1. Robert ide na konferenciju u Beograd?; Ide li Robert na konferenciju u Beograd?; Da li Robert ide na konferenciju u Beograd?
2. Marko ostaje u Beogradu jednu noć?; Ostaje li Marko u Beogradu jednu noć?; Da li Marko ostaje u Beogradu jednu noć?
3. Marko ima prijatelje u Beogradu?; Ima li Marko prijatelje u Beogradu?; Da li Marko ima prijatelje u Beogradu?
4. Avion kasni pola sata?; Kasni li avion pola sata?; Da li avion kasni pola sata?
5. Marko, Jelena i Robert stižu u Beograd na vreme?; Stižu li Marko, Jelean i Robert u Beograd na vreme?; Da li Marko, Jelena i Robert stižu u Beograd na vreme?

1. Ko ide na konferenciju u Beograd?; Gde Robert ide na konferenciju?
2. Ko ostaje u Beogradu jednu noć?; Koliko Marko ostaje u Beogradu?; Gde Marko ostaje jednu noć?
3. Ko ima prijatelje u Beogradu?; Šta Marko ima u Beogradu?; Gde Marko ima prijatelje?
4. Ko/šta kasni pola sata?; Koliko avion kasni?
5. Ko stiže u Beograd na vreme?; Gde Marko, Jelena i Robert stižu na vreme?

IV.

	sing.	*pl.*	*sing.*	*pl.*	*sing.*	*pl.*
Nom.	profesor	profesori	sok	sokovi	kafa	kafe
Gen.	profesora	profesora	soka	sokova	kafe	kafa
Acc.	profesora	profesore	sok	sokove	kafu	kafe
Instr.	profesorom	profesorima	sokom	sokovima	kafom	kafama
Prep.	profesoru	profesorima	soku	sokovima	kafi	kafama

Nom.	stjuardesa	stjuardese	pivo	piva	selo	sela
Gen.	stjuardese	stjuardesa	piva	piva	sela	sela
Acc.	stjuardesu	stjuardese	pivo	piva	selo	sela
Instr.	stjuardesom	stjuardesama	pivom	pivima	selom	selima
Prep.	stjuardesi	stjuardesama	pivu	pivima	selu	selima

Lesson Five

I.

1. Marko odseda u hotelu Slavija.
2. Robert i Jelena odsedaju kod Jeleninih roditelja.
3. Jelenin brat čeka Roberta i Jelenu na aerodromu.
4. Robert i Jelena idu u Skadarliju večeras.
5. Marko će se pridružiti Robertu i Jeleni.

II.

1. Je li taksi na aerodromu vrlo skup?; Da li je taksi na aerodromu vrlo skup?; Šta je vrlo skupo* na aerodromu?; Gde je taksi vrlo skup?

2. Hoćete li mi dozvoliti da vas pozovem na piće?; Da li ćete mi dozvoliti da vas pozovem na piće?; Šta ćete mi dozvoliti?; Gde ćete mi dozvoliti da vas pozovem?; (Kada ćete mi dozvoliti da vas pozovem na piće?)

3. Možete li nam se pridružiti na večeri?; Da li možete da nam se pridružite na večeri?; (Kada nam se možete pridružiti na večeri?; Gde nam se možete pridružiti na večeri?)

4. Je li Skadarlija Robertovo omiljeno mesto?; Da li je Skadarlija Robertovo omiljeno mesto?; (Kako se zove Robertovo omiljeno mesto?; Gde je Robertovo omiljeno mesto?)

5. Ima li dovoljno prostora u kolima?; Da li ima dovoljno prostora u kolima?; Gde ima dovoljno mesta?; Koliko ima mesta u kolima?

*The interrogative pronoun *šta* always takes the adjective in the neuter gender: Šta je skupo? Šta je lepo?, etc.

N.B. Questions in parentheses are made up on the basis of the original statement.

III.

	sing.	pl.	sing.	pl.	sing.	pl.
Nom.	stvar	stvari	večera	večere	mesto	mesta
Gen.	stvari	stvari	večere	večera	mesta	mesta
Dat.	stvari	stvarima	večeri	večerama	mestu	mestima
Acc.	stvar	stvari	večeru	večere	mesto	mesta
Voc.*	(stvari!	stvari!)	(večero!	večere!)	(mesto!	mesta!)
Instr.	stvari	stvarima	večerom	večerama	mestom	mestima
Prep.	stvari	stvarima	večeri	večerama	mestu	mestima

*The vocative is discussed in the following lesson.

N.B. Even when the genitive plural of a noun is spelled the same as the genitive singular and the nominative plural, the pronunciation is not the same; the penultimate vocal is lengthened in the genitive plural.

Nom.	makaze	vrata
Gen.	makaza	vrata
Dat.	makazama	vratima

Acc.	makaze	vrata
Voc.	makaze!	vrata!
Instr.	makazama	vratima
Prep.	makazama	vratima

IV.

Present

pozovem	pozovemo	odmorim se	odmorimo se
pozoveš	pozovete	odmoriš se	odmorite se
pozove	pozovu	odmori se	odmore se

Future

pozvaću	pozvaćemo	odmoriću se	odmorićemo se
pozvaćeš	pozvaćete	odmorićeš se	odmorićete se
pozvaće	pozvaće	odmoriće se	odmoriće se

Lesson Six

I.

1. Marko nije bio u Jugoslaviji dve godine.
2. Da, Robert je stranac.
3. Ne, Jelena nije strankinja.
4. Jelena čeka prtljag sa Markom.
5. Robert je otišao po kolica.
6. Marka su zadržali na pasoškoj kontroli zato što ima dvojno državljanstvo.
7. Robert ima samo lični laptop.
8. Marko ima samo lični foto-aparat.
9. Jelenin brat se zove Vlada.
10. Marko je upoznao Vladu.

II.

1. Avion je sleteo.
2. Nadali smo se.
3. Prošli ste.
4. Robert je mislio da je sve u redu.
5. Video (-la) sam Beograd.

6. Jelena je pila kafu.
7. Jelena, Robert i Marko su čekali.
8. Robert je upoznao Vladu i Marka.

III.
1. Da li je (Jeste li) avion sleteo? Avion nije sleteo.
2. Da li smo (Jesmo li se) nadali? Nismo se nadali.
3. Da li ste (Jeste li) prošli? Niste prošli.
4. Da li je (Jeste li) Robert mislio da je sve u redu? Robert nije mislio da je sve u redu.
5. Jesam li (Da li sam) video (-la) Beograd? Nisam video (-la) Beograd.
6. Da li je (Jeste li) Jelena pila kafu? Jelena nije pila kafu.
7. Da li su (Jesu li) Jelena, Robert i Marko čekali? Jelena, Robert i Marko nisu čekali.
8. Da li je (Jeste li) Robert upoznao Vladu i Marka? Robert nije upoznao Vladu i Marka.

IV.

Imperative

—	sedimo	—	pišimo
sedi	sedite	piši	pišite
(neka) sedi	(neka) sede	(neka) piše	(neka) pišu

—	znajmo	—	nadajmo se
znaj	znajte	nadaj se	nadajte se
(neka) zna	(neka) znaju	(neka) se nada	(neka) se nadaju

—	nadjimo	—	letimo
nadji	nadjite	leti	letite
(neka) nadje	(neka) nadju	(neka) leti	(neka) lete

V.

Nom.	vaš	pasoš	vaši	pasoši
Gen.	vašeg	pasoša	vaših	pasoša
Dat.	vašem	pasošu	vašim	pasošima
Acc.	vaš	pasoš	vaše	pasoše
Voc.	—	pasoše	—	pasoši

Instr.	vašim	pasošem	vašim	pasošima
Prep.	vašem	pasošu	vašim	pasošima

Nom.	moja torba	moje torbe
Gen.	moje torbe	mojih torbi
Dat.	mojoj torbi	mojim torbama
Acc.	moju torbu	moje torbe
Voc.	moja torbo	moje torbe
Instr.	mojom torbom	mojim torbama
Prep.	mojoj torbi	mojim torbama

Nom.	tvoja godina	tvoje godine
Gen.	tvoje godine	tvojih godina
Dat.	tvojoj godini	tvojim godinama
Acc.	tvoju godinu	tvoje godine
Voc.	— godino	— godine
Instr.	tvojom godinom	tvojim godinama
Prep.	tvojoj godini	tvojim godinama

Lesson Seven

I.

1. Ako bude problema on će se javiti njemu i njoj.; Ako bude problema on će se javiti njima.; Ako bude problema on će im se javiti.
2. Njemu ne treba pomoć sa stvarima.
3. On lepo savetuje njega.; On ga lepo savetuje.
4. On će se videti sa njim i njom večeras.; On će se videti sa njima večeras.

II.

1. Ko će se javiti Robertu i Jeleni?; Kome će se Marko javiti?; (Kada će se Marko javiti Robertu i Jeleni?; Zašto će se Marko javiti Robertu i Jeleni?)
2. Kome treba jedna soba za večeras?; Šta Marku treba za večeras?; Koliko soba Marku treba za večeras?; Za kada Marku treba jedna

soba?; (Gde Marku treba jedna soba za večeras?; Zašto Marku treba jedna soba za večeras?)

3. Ko trenutno ne prima kreditnu karticu?; Koji hotel trenutno ne prima kreditnu karticu?; Šta hotel "Slavija" trenutno ne prima?; Kada hotel "Slavija" ne prima kreditnu karticu?; (Zašto hotel "Slavija" trenutno ne prima kreditnu karticu?; Koju karticu hotel "Slavija" trenutno ne prima?; Koliko dugo hotel "Slavija" ne prima kreditnu karticu?)

4. Gde je JAT-ov šalter?; Šta je na desnoj strani u pasažu?; Koji šalter je na desnoj strani u pasažu?; Na kojoj strani u pasažu je JAT-ov šalter?; (Zašto je JAT-ov šalter na desnoj strani u pasažu?; Koliko dugo je JAT-ov šalter na desnoj strani u pasažu?)

5. Ko će zameniti novac po zvaničnom kursu?; Šta će Marko zameniti po zvaničnom kursu?; Po kom kursu će Marko zameniti novac?; (Kada će Marko zameniti novac . . .?; Gde će Marko zameniti novac?; Zašto će Marko zameniti novac po zvaničnom kursu?)

6. Ko će se videti večeras sa Robertom i Jelenom u Skadarliji?; Sa kim će se Marko videti večeras u Skadarliji?; Gde će se Marko videti sa Robertom i Jelenom večeras?; Kada će se Marko videti sa Robertom i Jelenom u Skadarliji?; (Zašto će se Marko videti sa Robertom i Jelenom u Skadarliji?)

7. Zašto je Marko srećan?; Ko je srećan zato što će se videti sa njima večeras?

8. Koliko dugo Marko nije bio u Beogradu?; Koliko godina Marko nije bio u Beogradu?; Ko nije bio u Beogradu dve godine?; Gde Marko nije bio dve godine?; (Zašto Marko nije bio u Beogradu dve godine?)

III.

Past		Present	
javio sam se	javili smo se	javljam se	javljamo se
javio si se	javili ste se	javljaš se	javljate se
javio se*	javili su se	javlja se	javljaju se

Future		Imperative	
javiću se	javićemo se	—	javimo se
javićeš se	javićete se	javi se	javite se
javiće se	javiće se	(neka) se javi	(neka) se jave

*Reflexive verbs in the past tense do not require the auxiliary verb in the third-person singular.

Past		Present	
služio sam	služili smo	služim	služimo
služio si	služili ste	služiš	služite
služio je	služili su	služi	služi

Future		Imperative	
služiću	služićemo	—	služimo
služićeš	služićete	služi	služite
služiće	služiće	(neka) služi	(neka) služe

Past		Present	
platio sam	platili smo	plaćam	plaćamo
platio si	platili ste	plaćaš	plaćate
platio je	platili su	plaća	plaćaju

Future		Imperative	
platiću	platićemo	—	platimo
platićeš	platićete	plati	platite
platiće	platiće	(neka) plati	(neka) plate

Past		Present	
pitao sam	pitali smo	pitam	pitamo
pitao si	pitali ste	pitaš	pitate
pitao je	pitali su	pita	pitaju

Future		Imperative	
pitaću	pitaćemo	—	pitajmo
pitaćeš	pitaćete	pitaj	pitajte
pitaće	pitaće	(neka) pita	(neka) pitaju

Past		Present	
izašao sam	izašli smo	izadjem	izadjemo
. . .	. . .	. . .	. . .

Future		Imperative	
izaći ću	izaći ćemo	—	izadjimo . . .

Past		Present	
skrenuo sam	skrenuli smo	skrenem	skrenemo
. . .	. . .	. . .	. . .

Future		Imperative	
skrenuću	skrenućemo	—	skrenimo . . .

Past		Present	
nastavio sam	nastavili smo	nastavljam	nastavljamo
. . .	. . .	. . .	. . .

Future		Imperative	
nastaviću	nastavićemo	—	nastavimo
. . .	. . .	. . .	. . .

Past		Present	
nameravao sam	nameravali smo	nameravam	nameravamo
. . .	. . .	. . .	. . .

Future		Imperative	
nameravaću	nameravaćemo	—	nameravajmo
. . .	. . .	. . .	. . .

Past		Present	
menjao sam	menjali smo	menjam	menjamo
. . .	. . .	. . .	. . .

Future		Imperative	
menjaću	menjaćemo	—	menjajmo
. . .	. . .	. . .	. . .

Past		Present	
savetovao sam	savetovali smo	savetujem	savetujemo
. . .	. . .	. . .	. . .

Future		Imperative	
savetovaću	savetovaćemo	—	savetujmo
. . .	. . .	. . .	. . .

IV.

Nom.	jednokrevetna soba	jednokrevetne sobe
Gen.	jednokrevetne sobe	jednokrevetnih soba
Dat.	jednokrevetnoj sobi	jednokrevetnim sobama
Acc.	jednokrevetnu sobu	jednokrevetne sobe
Voc.	jednokrevetna sobo	jednokrevetne sobe
Instr.	jednokrevetnom sobom	jednokrevetnim sobama
Prep.	jednokrevetnoj sobi	jednokrevetnim sobama

Nom.	kreditna kartica	kreditne kartice
Gen.	kreditne kartice	kreditnih kartica
Dat.	kreditnoj kartici	kreditnim karticama
Acc.	kreditnu karticu	(as Nom. *pl.*)
Voc.	kreditna kartice	(as Nom. *pl.*)
Instr.	kreditnom karticom	(as Dat. *pl.*)
Prep.	(as Dat. *sing.*)	(as Dat. *pl.*)

Nom.	veliki restoran	veliki restorani
Gen.	velikog restorana	velikih restorana
Dat.	velikom restoranu	velikim restoranima
Acc.	veliki restoran	velike restorane
Voc.	veliki restorane	veliki restorani
Instr.	velikim restoranom	velikim restoranima
Prep.	velikom restoranu	velikim restoranima

Nom.	radno vreme	radna vremena
Gen.	radnog vremena	radnih vremena
Dat.	radnom vremenu	radnim vremenima
Acc.	radno vreme	radna vremena
Voc.	radno vreme	radna vremena

Instr.	radnim vremenom	radnim vremenima
Prep.	radnom vremenu	radnim vremenima

Lesson Eight

I.

1. Konobar je preporučio Karadjordjevu šniclu, mešano meso sa roštilja ćevape, pljeskavice i ražnjiće.
2. Od hrane za vegetarijance u restoranu ima gibanice, proje, raznih salata "urnebes" salate, "šopske" salate . . .
3. Robert i Jelena bi želeli Karadjordjevu šniclu.
4. A Marko je naručio porciju lignji sa krompirom i razne salate.
5. Za piće su naručili crno i belo vino i kiselu vodu. (Oni su naručili crno i belo vino i kiselu vodu za piće.)
6. Vlada nije sa njima jer (zato što) je na treningu večeras.
7. U Beogradu, cene cigara se kreću do tri evra.
8. Marko se vraća kući krajem juna.

II.

1. Ne mogu (ništa) više da (po)jedem. Baš (zaista) sam sit.
2. Koliko ste visoki? (Koliko si visok,-a?)
3. Kada ste rodjeni? (Kada si rodjen,-a?)
4. Koliko košta let do Beograda?
5. Šta nam možete preporučiti (za jelo) od hrane?
6. Možete li nam, molim vas, doneti račun?
7. Gde mogu da kupim sveže povrće?
8. Čim se vratim kući moram da idem na posao.
9. Šta više (volite) voliš tenis ili fudbal?
10. Zar ste već stigli?

III.

Past		Present		Future	
uzeo sam	uzeli smo	uzmem	uzmemo	uzeću	uzećemo
uzeo si	uzeli ste	uzmeš	uzmete	uzećeš	uzećete
uzeo je	uzeli su	uzme	uzmu	uzeće	uzeće

Imperative		Potential	
—	uzmimo	uzeo bih	uzeli bismo
uzmi	uzmite	uzeo bi	uzeli biste
(neka) uzme	(neka) uzmu	uzeo bi	uzeli bi

Past		Present		Future	
rekao sam	rekli smo	reknem	reknemo	reći ću	reći ćemo
rekao si	rekli ste	rekneš	reknete	reći ćeš	reći ćete
rekao je	rekli su	rekne	reknu	reći će	reći će

Imperative		Potential	
—	recimo*	rekao bih	rekli bismo
reci	recite	rekao bi	rekli biste
		rekao bi	rekli bi

*This is an exception, please remember it.

Past		Present		Future	
jeo sam	jeli smo	jedem	jedemo	ješću	ješćemo
jeo si	jeli ste	jedeš	jedete	ješćeš	ješćete
jeo je	jeli su	jede	jedu	ješće	ješće

Imperative		Potential	
—	jedimo	jeo bih	jeli bismo
jedi	jedite	jeo bi	jeli biste
		jeo bi	jeli bi

Past		Present		Future	
voleo sam	voleli smo	volim	volimo	voleću	volećemo
voleo si	voleli ste	voliš	volite	volećeš	volećete
voleo je	voleli su	voli	vole	voleće	voleće

Imperative		Potential	
—	volimo	voleo bih	voleli bismo
voli	volite	voleo bi	voleli biste
		voleo bi	voleli bi

Past
kretao sam se	kretali smo se
kretao si se	kretali ste se
kretao se	kretali su se

Present
krećem se	krećemo se
krećeš se	krećete se
kreće se	kreću se

Future
kretaću se	kretaćemo se
kretaćeš se	kretaćete se
kretaće se	kretaće se

Imperative
—	krećimo se
kreći se	krećite se
neka se kreće	neka se kreću

Potential
kretao bih se	kretali bismo se
kretao bi se	kretali biste se
kretao bi se	kretali bi se

Past
dao sam	dali smo
dao si	dali ste
dao je	dali su

Present
dam	damo
daš	date
da	daju

Future
daću	daćemo
daćeš	daćete
daće	daće

Imperative
—	dajmo
daj	dajte

Potential
dao bih	dali bismo
dao bi	dali biste
dao bi	dali bi

GLOSSARY

Serbo-Croat–English

A

a	and, but
adresa	address
aerodrom	airport
ako	if
ali	but
američki	American
Amerika	America
Amerikanac	American man
Amerikanka	American woman
atmosfera	atmosphere
autobus	bus
avion	plane

B

bar	at least
bar	bar
baš	(a particle used for emphasis)
belo vino	white wine
beo,-a,-o (def. adj.: beli)	white
bez	without
bez leda	without ice
bih	("would like," a present perfect form of the verb "to be" used to express willingness)
biti	to be
blizu (adv.)	near, close
bolje (adv.)	better
brat	brother
broj	number
broj telefona	telephone number
brinuti se (Cl. 3)	to worry
budite (imperative, 2nd p. pl.)	be!

C

car	tsar
carina (fem.)	customs

carinik (masc.)	customs officer
celi,-a,-o	whole
cena (ijek.: cijena)	price
cigareta	cigarette
crn,-a,-o	black
Crna Gora	Montenegro
crno vino	red wine (lit.: black wine)
crven,-a,-o	red

Č

čaj	tea
čak	even
čaša (n.)	glass
čekati (Cl. 5)	to wait
često (adv.)	often
četiri	four
čim	as soon as

Ć

ćerka	daughter
ćevap	rolled finger of minced meat, grilled
ćup	jug

D

da	yes
da (with a verb)	to
dakle	so, therefore
da li	(question marker)
dan	day
dati	to give
(Cl. 5: dam, daš, da . . .)	
deset	ten
desni,-a,-o	right
dete (nom. pl. deca)	child
dezert	dessert
direktan,-na,-no	direct
divan,-a,-o	wonderful
do	to, until

dobar,-a,-o	good
dobro	well, good, OK, all right
dobrodošli	welcome
doći	to arrive, to come
(Cl. 1, dodjem . . .)	
dodati	to add
(Cl. 5, dodam, dodaš . . .)	
dogovor	arrangement
dogovoriti se	to agree, to make an arrangement
dok	while
dom	home
doneti	to bring
(Cl. 1, donesem,	
doneseš, donese . . .)	
doručak	breakfast
do skoro	until recently
dovoljno	enough
dozvoliti	to allow
dozvoljen,-a,-o	allowed
drago mi je	pleased to meet you
dva,-e,-a	two
(ijek.: dva, dvije, dva)	
dvadeset osmi,-a,-o	28th
dvojno državljanstvo	double citizenship
dvokrevetna soba	double room (lit.: a two-bed room)

DŽ
džez	jazz

DJ
djak	pupil, schoolchild

E
eho	echo
ekonomista	economist, accountant
Engleska	England
engleski	English
Englez	English man
Engleskinja	English woman

eno	there's
evo	here's
evro	euro

F

flaša	bottle
foto-aparat (masc.)	camera
Francuskinja	French woman
Francuz	Frenchman
fudbal	football
funta	pound

G

gde	where
gibanica	savory cheese pie made with filo-pastry, cottage cheese and eggs
gladan,-na,-no	hungry
gledati (Cl. 5)	to look, to watch
godina	year
gori (adv.)	worse
gospodin	gentleman
gost	guest
govoriti (Cl. 6)	to speak

H

hajdemo	let's go
hleb	bread
hotel	hotel
hrana	food
hrvatski	Croatian
hteti	to want
(irr. verb: hoću, hoćeš . . .)	
hvala	thank you

I

i	and
ići (Cl. 1: idem . . .)	to go
ili	or
ima	there is

imati (Cl. 5)	to have
ime (nom. pl.: imena)	name
informatika	information science, IT
i onako	anyway
iz	from
izaći (Cl. 1)	to come out, to go out
izlaz	exit
izvini / izvinite	excuse me
izvolite	please, here you are

J

JAT (jugoslovenski aero transport)	Yugoslav Air Transport
javiti (se) (Cl. 6)	to inform, to get in touch
jedan,-a,-o	one
jednokrevetna soba	single room (lit.: a one-bed room)
jelovnik	menu
jer	because
jesti	to eat
(Cl 1., jedem, jedeš, jede . . .)	
jezik	language, tongue
još	more
još uvek	still
juče	yesterday
jug	south
Jugosloven/i	Yugoslav/s
jun	June
jutro	morning

K

kad	when
kafa	coffee
kako se kaže . . .	how do you say . . .
Karadjordjeva šnicla	rolled, breaded veal cutlet, stuffed with cheese
kasniti	to be late
kasno (adv.)	late
kisela voda	sparkling mineral water (lit.: sour water)

ključ	key
knjiga	book
kofer	suitcase
koji,-a,-e	which, what
kola (pl. tantum)	car
kolač	cake
kolica (pl. tantum)	baggage cart, trolley
koliko	how much, (how long)
konferencija	conference
konobar	waiter
košarkaš	basketball player
koštati (Cl. 5)	to cost
kraj	end
krajem	at the end, by the end
kreditna kartica	credit card
krenuti (Cl. 3)	to come, to set off
kretati se	to move, to range (for prices)
(Cl. 2, krećem se, krećeš se . . .)	
krompir	potato
kuda	where, where to
kupatilo (neut.)	bathroom
kupiti (Cl. 6)	to buy
kurs	exchange rate
kutija	box, packet

L

lak,-a,-o	light
lav	lion
led	ice
lep,-a,-o	pretty, nice, beautiful
lekar	doctor, general practitioner, physician
let	flight
leteti (Cl. 6)	to fly
levi,-a,-o	left
ličan,-a,-o	personal
lignje	squid
loš,-a,-e	bad

LJ

ljubav	love
ljudi (pl. of čovek–man)	people

M

mali,-a,-o	small
malo	little
mama	mom
menjati (Cl. 5)	to change
mesec (ijek: mjesec)	month
meso	meat
mesto	place
mešan,-a,-o	mixed
minut	minute
misliti (Cl. 6)	to think
mnogo	much
moći	to be able to
(Cl. 1, mogu . . .)	
moj,-a,-e	my
molim	please (asking)
morati (Cl. 5)	to have to, must
more	sea, seaside
možda	maybe
može	it is possible (also: it is acceptable)
muzika	music

N

na	on, onto
na nas (acc.) je red	it's our turn
naći (Cl. 1)	to find
nadati se (Cl. 5)	to hope
najbolje (adv.)	best
nameravati (Cl. 5)	to intend
napojnica	tip
naravno (adv.)	of course
naručiti (Cl. 6)	to order
nastaviti (Cl. 6)	to continue
naš,-a,-e	our

nazad	back
ne	no
nedelja (Croatian: tjedan)	week
negde	somewhere
neko	somebody
nekoliko	several
nema problema	no problem
nema smisla	it's not fair (lit.: no meaning)
nemački,-a,-o	German
nikad(a)	never
nisam	I am not
nisam siguran	I'm not sure
ništa	nothing
niže	further down
njegov,-a,-o	his
Njujork	New York
noć (fem.)	night
nov,-a,-o	new
novac	money

O

oba,-e,-a (only pl.)	both
oblak	cloud
obično	usually
od	from
odakle	where from
odavde	from here
odbaciti	to give a lift, to give a ride
odlično	excellent
odmor	rest
odmoriti se (Cl. 6)	to take a rest
odsesti (Cl.1)	to stay
oko (nom. pl.: oči)	eye
oko (adv.)	around (followed by the genitive)
on	he
ona	she
ono	it
ono (adv.)	that (over there)

omiljen,-a,-o	favorite
onda	then
ostati (Cl. 3)	to stay
otići (Cl. 1)	to go, to depart
otpratiti (Cl. 6)	to see sbd off, to walk sbd somewhere
otprilike	roughly, approximately
ovaj,-a,-o	this
ovde	here
ovo (adv.)	this

P

pa	(a particle used like "well" or "then")
pasaž	passage
pasoš	passport
pasoška kontrola	passport control
pažljiv,-a,-o	careful
pepeljara	ashtray
persirati (Cl. 5)	to address someone formally, with a *vi* instead of *ti*
petak	Friday
petnaest	fifteen
pitati (Cl. 5)	to ask
piti (Cl. 4)	to drink
pivo	beer
plaćati (Cl. 5)	to pay
platiti (Cl. 6)	to pay
pljeskavica	(beef) burger
po	in, after, for
po	per
pola	half
polaziti (Cl. 6)	to depart, to leave, to set off
pomalo	(a) little
pomoć (fem.)	help
pomoći (Cl. 1)	to help
ponedeljak	Monday
porcija	portion
portir	porter
posada	crew

posao (masc.; nom. pl.: poslovi)	work
posle	after
poslovno	on business
pošta	post office / mail
poštovan	respected
povrće (coll. neut. n., no grammatical plural)	vegetables
pozvati (Cl. 2)	to invite, call up
pravo	straight, straightaway
preći (Cl. 1)	to go onto, to cross (over)
predstavništvo	office, agency
pregledati (Cl. 5)	to look through
preporučiti (Cl. 6)	to recommend
prezime (neut.)	surname
pridružiti se	to join
prijat-an,-na,-no	pleasant
prijatelj	friend
prijati	to be pleasant, enjoyable
prijaviti (Cl. 6)	to declare
prilika	chance, opportunity
primati (Cl. 5)	to receive
proći (Cl. 1)	to go through
profesor	teacher, lecturer, professor
proja	cornmeal (polenta) pastry with cheese and eggs
promeniti	change, exchange
propustiti (Cl. 6)	to miss
prostor	space
prtljag (coll. masc. n., no pl.)	luggage
prvo	first
puno	a lot
put	journey
putnik/putnici	passenger/s, traveler/s
putovati (Cl. 4)	to travel
pušenje	smoking
pušiti (Cl. 6)	to smoke

R

račun	bill
raditi	to do
radno vreme	working time, opening hours
razmeniti (Cl. 6)	to exchange, to swap
razni,-e,-o (only pl.)	various
razumeti (Cl. 5)	to understand
ražnjić	shish kebab
(mostly in pl.: ražnjići)	
red	order (also: queue)
recepcija	reception, counter, lobby
reći (Cl. 1)	to say
restoran	restaurant
retko (adv.)	seldom
riba	fish
rodbina (coll. fem. n.)	relatives
roditelj	parent
roštilj	barbecue, grill
ručak	lunch

S

s, sa	with
sa	from
sa ledom	with ice
sačekati (Cl. 5)	to wait for a while
sad, sada	now
salata	salad
sam,-a,-o	alone, on one's own
samo	only, just
saputnik	co-passenger
sat (also: čas - hour)	hour
sat	watch, clock
savetovati (Cl. 4)	to advise, to give advice
sedati (Cl. 5)	to be taking a seat
sedeti (Cl. 6)	to be sitting down
selo	village
se	(reflexive particle)
sesti (Cl. 1)	to sit down

sin (nom.pl.: sinovi)	son
sit,-a,-o	satiated, full
sitan novac	change (lit.: small money)
Skadarlija	(an old-fashioned street in Belgrade, with restaurants)
skrenuti (Cl. 3)	to turn
skup,-a,-o	expensive
Slavija	(a hotel in Belgrade, also a square and district in central Belgrade)
sleteti (Cl. 6)	to land (by plane)
slika	picture
slušati (cl. 5)	to listen
služiti (Cl. 6)	to serve
smeh	laughter
soba	room
sok od ananasa	pineapple juice
(sok od jabuke)	(apple juice)
(sok od pomorandže)	(orange juice)
specijalitet	specialty
srećan	happy
srpski	Serbian
srpskohrvatski	Serbo-Croatian
stići (Cl. 1, stižem . . .)	to arrive
stjuardesa	stewardess
strana	side
stranac	foreigner (male)
strankinja	foreigner (female)
stvar (fem.; nom. pl.: stvari)	thing
stvarno (adv.)	really
subota	Saturday
suprug (nom. pl.: supruzi)	husband
supruga (nom. pl.: supruge)	wife
sutra	tomorrow
svakako	by all means
sve (adv.)	everything
svež,-a,-e	fresh
svi,-e,-a (only pl.)	all, everybody
svoj,-a,-e	one's, yours

Š

šah	chess
šalter	counter, point
šećer	sugar
šnicla	cutlet
šopska salata	tomatoes, raw onions, and hot peppers topped with cottage cheese
šta	what
šteta	pity

T

tačan,-na,-no	exact
tačno na vreme	exactly on time
taj, ta, to	that
tako	that way
takodje (adv.)	too, also
taksi	taxi
tamo	over there
tašna	handbag
tata	dad
telefon	telephone
to	that
torba	bag
trafika	newsagent's, newsstand, kiosk
treba	it is necessary, it is needed
trening	training
trenutno	at the moment
tu	there / here
tvoj,-a,-e	your

U

u	in
u gotovini	in cash
u koliko sati	at what time
u pravu si	you are right
u redu	all right (lit.: in order)
ubediti (Cl. 6)	to persuade

učiti (Cl. 6)	to learn, to study
ugodan	comfortable
ulaz	entrance
ulica (n.)	street
ulični,-a,-o (adj.)	street
umoran	tired
umetnost (fem.)	art
upoznati (Cl. 5)	to introduce, to get to know, to meet
urnebes	chaos
urnebes salata	tomatoes, peppers, and cheese with spices made into a paste
ustvari	in fact
uvek	always
uzeti	to take
(Cl.1, uzmem, uzmeš . . .)	

V

vazduh	air
važi	OK, all right, agreed
večera	supper, dinner
večeras	tonight
već	already
vegetarijanac (n.)	vegetarian
verovatno	probably
veza	contact
vezati se (Cl. 2)	to tie oneself (to put the seat belt on)
videti (Cl. 6)	to see
visina	height
više	more
viza	visa
voćni sok	fruit juice
voda	water
voleti	to like, to love
(Cl. 6, volim, voliš, voli . . .)	
vratiti se (Cl. 6)	to return
vrlo	very
vrsta	kind, sort

Z

za	for, in, to
za mene	for me
za petnaest minuta	in fifteen minutes
zadržati (Cl. 6)	to keep
zaista	really, indeed
zašto	why
zašto da ne	why not?
zatim	then
zato što	because
zatvoren,-a,-o	closed
zatvoriti (Cl. 5)	to close
zavisiti (Cl. 6)	to depend
zdravo	hello
zemlja	country
znači	so, therefore (also: "it means" from "značiti")
znati	to know
zvanični,-a,-o	official

Ž

želeti	to wish
život	life
žuriti (Cl. 6)	to hurry, to be in a hurry

APPENDICES

Useful Phrases and Public Notices

Аутобуска станица	Autobuska stanica	Bus stop
Болница	Bolnica	Hospital
Дежурна служба	Dežurna služba	Officer on duty
Хитна помоћ	Hitna pomoć	Emergency (aid)
Информације	Informacije	Information
Издаје се	Izdaje se	For rent
Милиција	Milicija	Police
Не гази траву	Ne gazi travu	Don't walk on the grass
Не ради	Ne radi	Out of order / Doesn't work
На продају	Na prodaju	For sale
Нон-стоп	Non-stop	Non-stop
Обезбеђење	Obezbedjenje	Security
Отворено	Otvoreno	Open
Пажљиво	Pažljivo	Careful / Caution
Пажња	Pažnja	Attention
Пешачка зона	Pešačka zona	Pedestrian zone
Полиција	Policija	Police
Портир	Portir	Porter
Пошта	Pošta	Post office
Радно време	Radno vreme	Opening hours (Working hours)
Рецепција	Recepcija	Reception
Школа	Škola	School
Телефон	Telefon	Telephone
Улица . . .	Ulica . . .	. . . Street
Забрањен прилаз	Zabranjen prilaz	No access
Забрањен улаз	Zabranjen ulaz	No entrance
Забрањено пушење	Zabranjeno pušenje	No smoking
Затворено	Zatvoreno	Closed

Pesmica / **A Poem**

Ala je lep . . .

Ala je lep
ovaj svet,
onde potok,
ovde cvet;
tamo njiva,
ovde sad,
eno sunce,
evo hlad!
Tamo Dunav,
zlata pun,
onde trava,
ovde žbun.
Slavuj pesmom
ljulja lug.
Ja ga slušam
i moj drug.

—Jovan Jovanović Zmaj*

*Jovan Jovanović, nicknamed Zmaj, is a famous nineteenth-century Yugoslav poet. This ode is from his large oeuvre of children's poetry.

Vocabulary

ala	(particle for emphasis)
cvet	flower
drug	friend
Dunav	the Danube
ga (short of *njega*)	him, it (acc.)
hlad	shade
ljuljati (Cl. 5)	to swing
lug	wood
njiva	(wheat) field
onde	over there
ovaj	this
pesma	song
potok	stream
pun,-a,-o	full
sad	garden
slavuj	nightingale
slušati (Cl. 5)	to listen
sunce	sun, sunshine
svet	world
tamo	over there
trava	grass
zlato	gold
žbun	shrub, bush

Recept *Proja*

Proja je slano pecivo od kukuruznog brašna sa sirom. *Proja* se često služi kao dodatak ostalim jelima.

SASTOJCI:

2 jajeta
2 dl ulja (ili 1,5 dl ulja i 0,5 dl kisele vode)
2 dl jogurta
200 gr belog sira
7 kašika pšeničnog brašna
7 kašika kukuruznog brašna
1 kašičica soli
1 kašičica praška za pecivo

1. Umutite 2 jajeta.

2. Dodajte ulje, jogurt (i kiselu vodu, po želji) i promešajte.

3. Zatim, dodajte sir, brašno, so i prašak za pecivo i promešajte.

Smesa treba da bude glatka. Ukoliko je smesa suviše tvrda, dodajte vodu ili ulje. Pecite na srednjoj temperaturi oko pola sata, ili dok ne porumeni. Služite dok je još topla.

Za 4–6 osoba.

Recipe *Proja*

Proja is a savory pie made of corn flour with cottage cheese. *Proja* is often served as a side dish.

INGREDIENTS:

2 eggs
1 cup (200 ml) vegetable oil (or ⅔ cup (150 ml) oil and ⅓ cup (50 ml)
       sparkling water)
1 cup (200 ml) plain yogurt
7 ounces (200 gr) cottage cheese
⅔ cup (7 spoonfuls) plain flour
⅔ cup (7 spoonfuls) coarse yellow cornmeal
1 teaspoon salt
1 teaspoon baking powder

1. Whisk eggs.

2. Add oil (and sparkling water, if desired) and yogurt and mix together.

3. Add cheese, flour, salt, and baking powder and mix well.

The mass should be smooth. If the mass is too hard, add more sparkling water or oil. Bake at 350 degrees F. (medium temperature) for ½ hour, or until golden brown. Serve warm.

Serves 4–6.

Vocabulary

beli sir	cottage cheese, curd (lit.: white cheese)
brašno	flour
često	often
dl	deciliter (100 milliliters)
dodatak	addition
dodati	to add
dok	while
gladak, glatka, glatko	smooth
jaje (nom. pl.: jaja)	egg
jelo	dish
jogurt	yogurt
kao	like
kašičica	teaspoon
kašika	spoon
kukuruz	corn
kukuruzni,-a,-o (adj.)	corn
osoba (nom. pl.: osobe)	person (a feminine noun which applies to any gender)
ostali,-e,-a (pl. only)	the rest
pšenični,-a,-o (adj.)	wheat
pšenica	wheat
pecivo	pie
peći	to bake
pola	half
porumeneti	to become golden brown (lit.: red), also: to blush
prašak	powder
promešati	to mix together, to stir
sastojci	ingredients
sir	cheese
slan,-a,-o	savory (lit.: salty)
služiti	to serve
smesa	mass
so (fem.; nom. pl: soli)	salt
srednji,-a,-e	medium
suviše (adv.)	exceedingly

temperatura	temperature
topao, topla, toplo	warm
tvrd,-a,-o	hard
ukoliko (adv.)	if, in case
ulje (neut.)	oil
umutiti	to whisk
zatim	then

N.B. Notice that the instructions for making the dish are in the imperative. Instructions in cookbooks can appear either in the imperative or in the infinitive for a less personal effect.

ACKNOWLEDGMENTS

I'd like to thank Nick Awde for the initiative, support and advice; Hippocrene Books and Caroline Gates in particular for the tireless work, correspondence and encouragement; Vladan and Saška Rankov for all their time and for saving the work from my computer illiteracy, and Paul Heaney for pretending to be an American tourist, but chiefly, for being himself. Special thanks to my mum—who first taught me to appreciate my own language, and to my dad—who taught me to appreciate other languages.

From Hippocrene's Serbo-Croatian Library

SERBO-CROATIAN–ENGLISH/ ENGLISH–SERBO-CROATIAN PRACTICAL DICTIONARY

- Over 24,000 entries
- Completely modern and up-to-date
- Concise, easy-to-use format
- Appendices of Serbo-Croatian and English irregular verbs

24,000 entries • 400 pages • ISBN 0-7818-0445-0 • $16.95pb • (130)

Related Titles from Hippocrene...

CROATIAN-ENGLISH/ENGLISH-CROATIAN DICTIONARY & PHRASEBOOK

- Over 4,500 entries
- Pronunciation guide
- A basic grammar
- Essential phrases
- Ideal for travelers, students, business persons, and relief organizations

4,500 entries • 272 pages • 3¾ x 7½ • ISBN 0-7818-0810-3 • $11.95pb • (111)

SERBIAN-ENGLISH/ENGLISH-SERBIAN CONCISE DICTIONARY

- Over 7,500 entries
- Phonetic spellings
- Pronunciation guide

7,500 entries • 394 pages • 4 x 6 • ISBN 0-7818-0556-2 • $14.95 • (326)

BOSNIAN-ENGLISH/ENGLISH-BOSNIAN CONCISE DICTIONARY

• Over 8,500 entries
• Compact and easy to use
• Commonsense pronunciation guides for Bosnian and English speakers

8,500 entries • 331 pages • 4 x 6 • ISBN 0-7818-0276-8 • $14.95 • (329)

BOSNIAN-ENGLISH/ENGLISH-BOSNIAN DICTIONARY & PHRASEBOOK

• Over 3,100 entries
• Essential phrases for getting around the city and the country
• Ideal for tourists, business travelers, and relief organizations

3,100 entries • 171 pages • 3¾ x 7½ • ISBN 0-7818-0596-1 • $11.95 • (691)

Prices subject to change without prior notice. **To order Hippocrene Books,** contact your local bookstore, call (718) 454-2366, or write to: Hippocrene Books, 171 Madison Ave. New York, NY 10016. Please enclose check or money order adding $5.00 shipping (UPS) for the first book and $.50 for each additional title.